Knit Vintage

More than 20 patterns for starlet sweaters & other knitwear from the 1930s, 1940s & 1950s

Madeline Weston & Rita Taylor

Photography by Debi Treloar

jacqui small

Contents

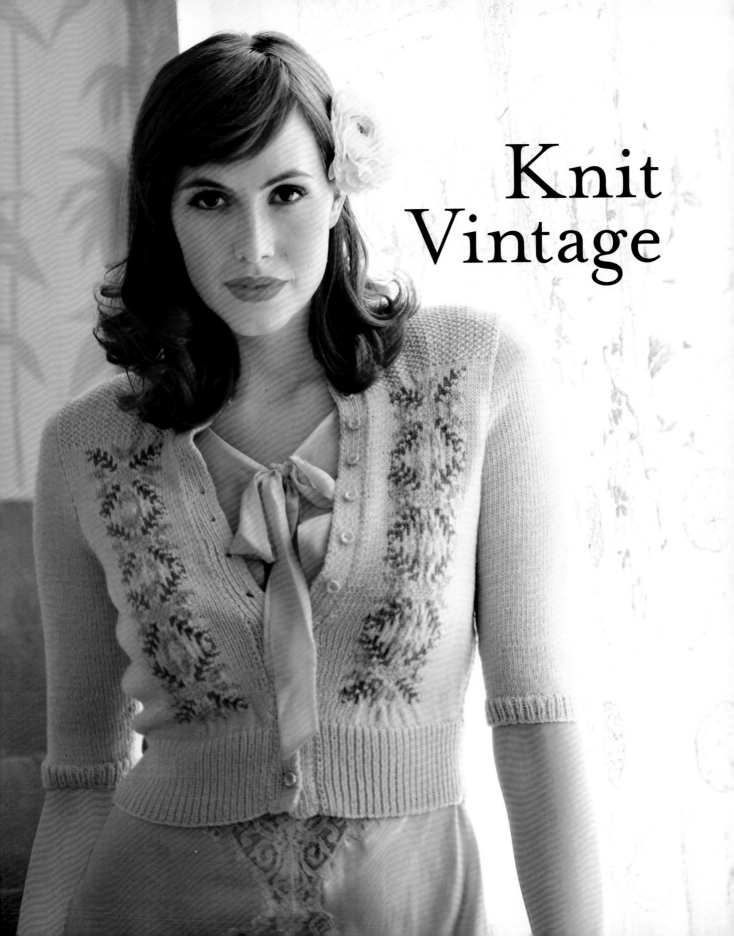

Knit
Vintage

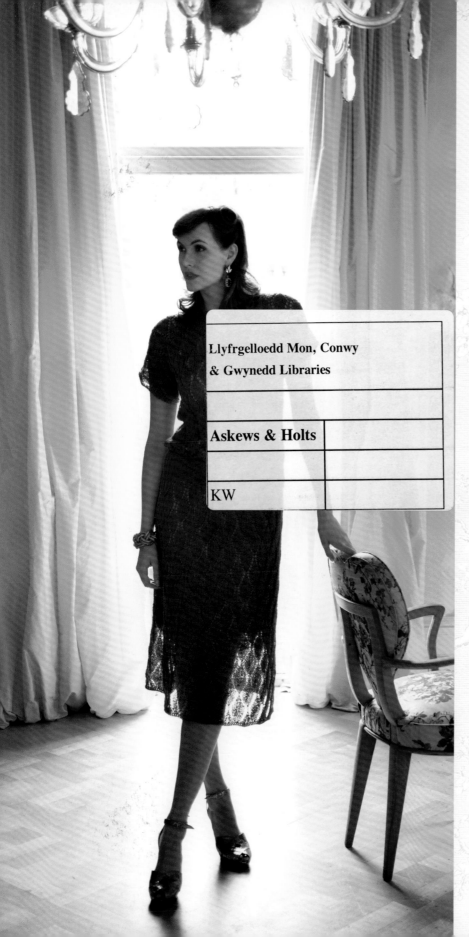

First published in 2012 by **Jacqui Small LLP**
An imprint of Aurum Press Ltd
7 Greenland Street
London NW1 0ND

ISBN: 978 1 906417 66 6

A catalogue record for this book is available
from the British Library.

2014 2013 2012
10 9 8 7 6 5 4 3 2 1

Printed in China

Publisher Jacqui Small
Managing Editor Kerenza Swift
Commissioning Editor Zia Mattocks
Art Director Barbara Zuñiga
Production Peter Colley

Stylist Marianne Cotterill
Hair and Make-up Victoria Barnes

Models Nevs Models: Juliana Aneli, Nathalie
Cox and Tillie; BMA: Jessica Munro

Location www.mapesburyroad.com

Introduction

Knit Vintage aims to bring you a beautiful selection of patterns from the 1930s, 1940s and 1950s, updated using modern yarns and sized for modern women. It is interesting to look back at how fashion – and knitting – changed over this period.

Home knitting was widely practised during this time, and published knitting patterns, which had existed from late in the nineteenth century, became more widespread. However, it took the fashion designers Coco Chanel and Elsa Schiaparelli to bring knitting into the realm of high fashion. The queen of glamorous knitwear was Elsa Schiaparelli, who was more avant-garde than Coco Chanel, the favourite of the late 1920s and early 1930s. Schiaparelli, who promoted glamour over comfort, started as a knitwear designer and then moved into mainstream fashion where she had enormous influence over the styles of her day. Perhaps her most famous knitted sweater was the one with the huge intarsia bow at the neck, which has been copied many times over the years.

The look of the 1930s moved away from the boyish figure that was so in vogue in the 1920s, into a silhouette that showed off the feminine form. The accent was on glamour, with the bust and waist in their natural places and the garments being more figure-hugging. Sweaters were sometimes worn tucked in to the skirt, which again emphasized the waist; some styles had the waist set higher than normal in order to make the legs appear longer. Emphasis was placed on the neckline with collars and bows; puffed sleeves and shoulder pads were much in evidence, to make the hips and waist appear more slender, and skirts fell to mid-calf to give the desired tall and slim outline. Ruffles and pleats embellished simpler shapes and accentuated femininity.

After the stock-market crash of 1929, women turned to knitting to copy the styles worn by popular film stars at a fraction of the cost. Hollywood became the dictator of fashion trends and by the late 1930s women everywhere were emulating their favourite stars. The proliferation of magazines and knitting patterns meant that women could be fashionable without having to spend a fortune. Women knitted everything from skirts and dresses to suits and jackets, and followed the advice on fashion shapes, yarns and colours in their favourite magazines. The competition between knitting-pattern publishers fed the desire for exciting styles, and knitting became a craze. Towards the end of the 1930s new yarns and colours were becoming more common, providing a much wider choice for knitters.

In the 1940s, and particularly during the war years, designs and shapes became more sober, and everyone was encouraged to 'make do and mend'. The lines became much more tailored, more practical and less extravagant; jackets and skirts were shorter, but still with a defined waist, often with a belt, and trousers for women became more popular.

Fashion designers adjusted to the restrictions by producing more military, square shoulders. Lace knitting was popular because the finer the yarn, the more knitting could be produced, and also because the factories creating lace before the war had been taken over for the manufacture of munitions. During the war, wool was needed for the fabric used by the services and yarn was rationed in the UK, so it was vital to make things in a very economical way. Fair Isle-type patterns were popular because small oddments of different colours could be used up in the multicoloured designs.

However, during the Second World War women were still determined to appear fashionable and attractive, and knitting remained enormously popular, with printed patterns designed to use the allowed yarn to maximum effect. Sleeveless and short-sleeved sweaters that could be worn with the smart 'costume', or suit, were the vogue, as were lacy knits that would feminize the rather masculine shapes that were prevalent. Collars and cuffs might be added to plain sweaters, buttons became more decorative, and costume-jewellery clips and brooches might adorn a simple neckline in order to add a pretty detail to a more practical style.

Throughout the 1930s and 1940s, textured stitches played an important part in single-colour designs, with puffed sleeves and square necks continuing to be popular. If there was no collar on the design, the yoke was sometimes knitted in a contrasting, more decorative stitch to give emphasis to the neckline.

Folk art and 'peasant' motifs became the fashion in the late 1940s, with flowers, figures and stars adorning the neckline or front of sweaters and cardigans. These were often termed Tyrolean or Scandinavian, and could incorporate bobbles and neck ties as well as the coloured motifs that would be knitted in, or embroidered.

The twinset of matching sweater and cardigan became hugely popular, often with a short-sleeved sweater that was more economical with yarn. This was a style that proved to be enormously long lived, and in the 1950s twinsets were worn right across the social scale – by women going to work and by Hollywood stars such as Audrey Hepburn and Grace Kelly.

The 1950s saw Dior's New Look become accepted, with much more fabric being used in its full, longer skirts. This, too, was the era of the 'sweater girl' and a completely different shape of underwear that emphasized and exaggerated the bust. The bolero overtook the cardigan, often embellished with beads for the evening, and dressy sweaters decorated with sequins or embroidery also became fashionable as evening wear.

After the war luxury yarns began to appear and the knitting industry expanded; factories that had been engaged in the war effort now produced a huge range of new yarns. Angora and cashmere were fashionable, and man-made fibres were being produced to blend with the new yarns. This, and new dyeing techniques, meant that the previous restricted colour choice was overtaken by a proliferation of shades and types of yarn for the hand-knitter. Metallic yarns and acrylic yarns were among the innovations, and knitters had a vast choice of different materials. Yarn companies all produced a range of patterns to be used in conjunction with these yarns. Knitting was considered an important skill and was often taught in schools. Knitwear was still enormously popular throughout the 1950s. Chunky cardigans and more casual sweaters were worn as part of the new sportier style of women's fashion, and stoles gradually replaced boleros for evening wear.

Vintage Details

Your choice of buttons, beads and colours can make a huge difference to the look of the final garment. Buttons were often used to embellish a sweater when they had no function: the *Jayne* Button-Front Top (see page 16) is an example of such a garment. Set tiny buttons close together or slightly larger ones further apart and you will create an entirely different look. The appearance of the *Hedy* Tyrolean-Pattern Cardigan (see page 46) will change, depending on whether you use colour-matched buttons or contrasting ones; natural horn would be a good choice on this cardigan. If you are using beads, make sure they are not too heavy, or they will drag the garment down. Lots of tiny beads, rather than a few larger ones, make a sparkling effect on the *Ava* Angora Bolero (see page 52), which could be straight out of an early 1950s movie.

As well as being functional, buttons also give interest to the back of a neckline. The *Vivien* Fair Isle-Style Sweater from the 1940s (see page 70) shows the then fashionable use of buttons along the shoulder, a style that was copied from fishermen's knits.

Look for buttons in antique markets and second-hand shops and you can be sure that your choice will make your garment absolutely unique.

HINTS FOR KNITTING THE PATTERNS IN THIS BOOK

* Some patterns have a lot of shaped increases in the body. Ribs were tighter on the body, so the number of stitches cast on is not indicative of the final width of the bust (see *Wallis* Pleated Cardigan, page 60).

* When you are joining sleeves, be sure to join the shoulder seams first and then ease in the fullness of the sleeve cap – especially important if the style is a slightly puffed sleeve.

* In some of the patterns, such as the cardigan that is part of the *Barbara* Fine Cable Twinset (see page 96), the back is narrower and the front is more full, meaning that the armhole is not the same on the back and front, so that the sleeve seams are set towards the front of the side seams. This is noted in the finishing section of the pattern.

CONVERTING VINTAGE PATTERNS

If you are lucky enough to have vintage patterns that you would like to knit, you may find this information about substituting yarns useful.

Bear in mind that until just a few years ago, the length of the yarn was not given in the pattern, and in a lot of cases there was not even a specified weight as we know it now, but the amount was stated in skeins. Also, until Britain adopted metric weights as standard, British yarn was usually sold in 1oz balls – 1oz is approximately equivalent to 28g, so it is relatively easy to convert the weight. But what about the thickness of the yarn? The 'ply' of the yarn was not a guarantee that all manufacturers' yarns would knit up to the same tension, and some of them had names that gave no indication at all of the thickness of the yarn: 'bedjacket floss', 'wheeling', 'fingering' and 'super sport weight' would mean very little in today's yarn shops. In addition, yarns used in the 1930s and 1940s tended to be finer than those generally available today. However, lace-weight yarns are becoming much more widely available and it is worth seeking them out for vintage knitting patterns that specify fine wool.

As well as the yarns being different to modern yarns, old patterns were written for women who were generally smaller. The fit of the patterns differed from most of those we are used to now and the pattern was often only given in one size. The older patterns only give the most basic of measurements – for instance, simply bust size – there might well be no body or sleeve lengths given, and there are certainly no actual measurements. So, in order to find out the size of the finished garment, you have to do a few sums based on the quoted tension and the number of stitches that there are across the bust (many of the patterns from the 1930s and 1940s had a lot less stitches cast on at the waist and then increased gradually). Once you have done this sum and the garment seems to be the right fit for you, the next step is to knit some tension squares with different sized needles and different yarns until you get one as near as possible to the original. If you can get the correct number of stitches but the row count is wrong, try using a smaller needle for the purl rows.

If all this fails and you still can't get an exact copy of the pattern, the upside is that you are now halfway to designing your own using a vintage pattern as inspiration, which is when you will really be able to exercise your creativity.

Pretty Tops

This selection of pretty tops is typical of patterns that were published in their thousands towards the end of the 1940s and into the 1950s. The knitters who had knitted for the war effort were now able to turn their minds to making things for themselves, and they wanted pretty and feminine knitted tops that could take the place of blouses. They could be worn with simple tailored suits, pencil skirts or the slacks of the 1940s, as well as the new full skirts that were coming into style in the 1950s. The appeal of knitting for oneself – still true today – was in the extensive choice of yarns that enabled the fashion-conscious woman to select exactly the right shade to complement her favourite outfit. Choose a yarn that is comfortable next to the skin for these short-sleeved and sleeveless styles. Try a silk mixture, cotton or bamboo and they will be favourites all the year round.

A soft mercerized cotton makes this a perfect summer top, which will take you through the day and into the evening. The high rib accentuates the waist and the pretty collar gives a soft line to the V neck, both enhancing the top's feminine shape. The lace stitch is really simple to work, yet the final effect is sheer early 1950s glamour. The buttons are purely decorative, but they add the perfect finishing touch, so use the prettiest ones, or the best colour match, that you can find — the choice is yours.

Jayne Button-Front Top

Materials

YARN
8 [9, 10] x 50g balls Rowan Siena 4ply (100% mercerized cotton, approximately 140m/153 yards), shade 670 Sloe

NEEDLES
1 pair needles size 3mm
1 pair needles size 3.25mm
Stitch holder

NOTIONS
12 buttons, 1cm/½in in diameter

MEASUREMENTS
To fit Small [Medium, Large]
Actual chest size 90 [94, 99]cm
35 [37, 39]in
Length to back neck 53 [58, 63]cm
21 [23, 25]in

TENSION
28 stitches and 40 rows measure 10cm/4in over pattern on 3.25mm needles (or size needed to obtain given tension)

PATTERN
Row 1 *K1, yf, k2tog, k3, p1, k1, p1, rep from * to end.
Row 2 and every alt row P1, k1, *p8, k1, rep from * to last 7 sts, p1.
Row 3 *K2, yf, k2tog, k2, p1, k1, p1, rep from * to end.
Row 5 *K3, yf, k2tog, k1, p1, k1, p1, rep from * to end.
Row 7 *K4, yf, k2tog, p1, k1, p1, rep from * to end.
Row 8 As Row 2.
These 8 rows form the pattern.

FRONT
Using 3mm needles, cast on 110 [112, 116] sts.
Work in k1, p1 rib for 9 [10, 10]cm/3½ [4, 4]in, inc 7 sts across the last row as follows:
Small Rib 10, m1, (rib 15, m1) 6 times, rib 10.
Medium Rib 12, m1, (rib 22, m1) 4 times, rib 12.
Large Rib 10, m1, (rib 16, m1) 6 times, rib 10.
(117 [119, 123] sts.)
Change to 3.25mm needles and cont in patt as follows:
Next row Moss st 3 [4, 6], patt 39 sts, moss st 33, patt 39 sts, moss st 3 [4, 6].
Now cont in this way, keeping 2 panels of 39 sts in patt and rem sts in moss st, inc 1 st at both ends of every 8th row 4 [6, 6] times, working all inc sts in moss st, cont straight until work measures 30 [32, 34]cm/12 [12½, 13]in ending with a p row.

CAP SLEEVES
Cast on 9 sts at beg of next 2 rows.

NECK OPENING

Moss st 16 [19, 23], patt 39 sts, moss st 16, leave these sts on a stitch holder, cast off 1 st, moss st 16 including st already on needle, patt 39 sts, moss st to end.

Now cont on these sts keeping a panel of 39 sts in patt and rem sts in moss st until sleeve measures 17cm/7in, ending with RS facing.

SHAPE SHOULDERS

Taking care to keep the patt as set, cast off 6 sts at sleeve edge on every alt row 8 times, then 7 [10, 12] sts once. Work on rem sts in moss st for 6cm/2in. Cast off. Rejoin yarn to sts on holder and work the other side to match, reversing shapings.

BACK

Work as for front rib until inc row after rib border has been worked.

Next row Moss st 3 [4, 6], patt to last 3 [4, 6] sts, moss st 3 [4, 6].

Cont in this way keeping 111 sts in patt, inc 1 st at both ends of every 8th row 4 [6, 6] times, working all inc sts in moss st, then cont straight until work measures the same as front to cap sleeve.

CAP SLEEVES

Cast on 9 sts at beg of next 2 rows.

Then, keeping patt as set, cont until sleeve measures the same as front sleeve.

SHAPE SHOULDER

Cast off 6 sts at beg of next 16 rows, then 7 [10, 12] sts at beg of next 2 rows. Cast off.

FINISHING

Block or press carefully, as given on page 137.
Join side and shoulder seams.
Join ends of neckband using a flat seam, then sew band to back of neck.
Sew buttons on front of top as illustrated.

This early 1950s pattern for a short-sleeved top with pretty lace panels over the shoulders and down the sleeves, knitted in a luxurious blend of silk and wool, looks dressy with a pencil skirt or trousers, or retro with a full skirt or cut-off jeans. The hook and eye at the neck can be left undone or fastened to make a flattering keyhole opening.

Bette Top with Keyhole Neckline

Materials

YARN
3 x 100g balls Fyberspates Scrumptious 4ply (45% silk, 55% superwash merino, approximately 365m/400 yards), shade 308 Teal

NEEDLES
1 pair needles size 2.25mm
1 pair needles size 3mm

NOTIONS
1 small hook and eye

SPECIAL ABBREVIATION
sk2p slip 1, knit 2 together, pass slipped stitch over

MEASUREMENTS
To fit Small [Medium, Large]
Actual chest size 82 [87, 93]cm
32¼ [34¼, 36½]in
Length to back neck 47 [49, 52]cm
18½ [19¼, 20½]in
Underarm sleeve 11cm/4½in all sizes

TENSION
30 stitches and 40 rows measure 10cm/4in over pattern on 3mm needles (or size needed to obtain given tension)

Notes: Where one instruction is given it applies to all sizes. In this pattern knit stitches are sometimes given in sequence (for example, k1, k32, k1) to help the knitter break down the elements of the repeat and make the pattern easier to follow.

FRONT
Using 2.25mm needles, cast on 106 [114, 122] sts and work in k1, p1 rib for 10cm/4in. Change to 3mm needles and work as follows:
Row 1 P10 [14, 18], k2, (yf, k4, sk2p, k4, yf, k1) twice, k1, p32, k2, (yf, k4, sk2p, k4, yf, k1) twice, k1, p10 [14, 18].
Row 2 K10 [14, 18], p27, k32, p27, k10 [14, 18].
Row 3 P10 [14, 18], k3, (yf, k3, sk2p, k3, yf, k3) twice, p32, k3, (yf, k3, sk2p, k3, yf, k3) twice, p10 [14, 18].
Row 4 As row 2.
Row 5 P10 [14, 18], k1, k2tog, yf, k1, yf, k2, sk2p, k2, yf, k1, yf, sk2p, yf, k1, yf, k2, sk2p, k2, yf, k1, yf, skpo, k1, p32, k1, k2tog, yf, k1, yf, k2, sk2p, k2, yf, k1, yf, sk2p, yf, k1, yf, k2, sk2p, k2, yf, k1, yf, skpo, k1, p10 [14, 18].
Row 6 As row 2.
Row 7 K10 [14, 18], k1, yf, skpo, k2, yf, k1, sk2p, k1, yf, k3, yf, skpo, k2, yf, k1, sk2p, k1, yf, k2, k2tog, yf, k1, k32, k1, yf, skpo, k2, yf, k1, sk2p, k1, yf, k3, yf, skpo, k2, yf, k1, sk2p, k1, yf, k2, k2tog, yf, k10 [14, 18].
Row 8 Purl.
Row 9 K10 [14, 18], k2, (yf, sk2p, yf, k1) 6 times, k1, k32, k2, (yf, sk2p, yf, k1) 6 times, k10 [14, 18].
Row 10 Purl.
These 10 rows form the pattern.
Cont in patt, inc 1 st at each end of next and every foll 8th row until 126 [134, 142] sts are on needle.
Cont until work measures 32 [33, 34]cm/12½ [13, 13½]in.

SHAPE ARMHOLES AND NECK
With RS facing:

Row 1 Cast off 6 [7, 7] sts, p13 [16, 19], patt 27 sts, p12, cast off 8 sts, p11, patt 27 sts, p to end of row.
Row 2 Cast off 6 [7, 7] sts, k13 [16, 19], p27, k12, turn and cont on these 52 [55, 58] sts.
Row 3 P12, patt 27, p to end.
Row 4 Cast off 6 [7, 7] sts, k7 [9, 12], p27, k12.
Row 5 As row 3.
Cont in patt on these sts, dec 1 st at armhole edge on next and each alt row until 43 [45, 47] sts rem.
Cont in patt without shaping until work measures 43 [44.5, 46]cm/17 [17½, 18]in from beg.
Cont in patt, dec 1 st at neck edge on next and each alt row until 30 sts rem.
Cont in patt until work measures 47 [49, 52]cm/18½ [19½, 20½]in from beg.

SHAPE SHOULDER

With WS facing, and keeping patt as set:
Cast off 7 [9, 9] sts at beg of next and foll alt row and 8 [9, 9] sts at beg of foll 2 alt rows.
Return to rem sts, rejoin yarn at neck edge and complete to match first side, reversing shaping.

BACK

Using 2.25mm needles, work 10cm/4in rib as for front. Change to 3mm needles.
Row 1 Purl.
Row 2 Knit.
Rep rows 1 and 2 twice.
Row 7 Knit.
Row 8 Purl.
Rep rows 7 and 8 once.
These 10 rows form the pattern.
Cont in patt, inc 1 st at each end of next and every foll 8th row until 126 [134, 142] sts are on needle.
Cont until work measures same as front to armholes.
Cast off 6 [7, 7] sts at beg of next 4 rows then dec 1 st at each end of alt rows to 94 [106, 110] sts.
Cont until back measures same as front to shoulders.

SHAPE SHOULDERS

Cast off 7 [9, 9] sts at beg of next 4 rows and 8 [9, 9] sts at beg of foll 4 rows.
Leave rem 34 [34, 38] sts on a spare needle.

SLEEVES

Using 3mm needles, cast on 87 [91, 97] sts.
Next row Knit.
Next row Purl.
Work in patt as follows:

Row 1 P30 [32, 35], k2, (yf, k4, sk2p, k4, yf, k1) twice, k1, p30 [32, 35].
Row 2 K30 [32, 35], p27, k30 [32, 35].
Row 3 P30 [32, 35], k3, (yf, k3, sk2p, k3, yf, k3) twice, p30 [32, 35].
Row 4 As row 2.
Row 5 P30 [32, 35], k1, k2tog, yf, k1, yf, k2, sk2p, k2, yf, k1, yf, sk2p, yf, k1, yf, k2, sk2p, k2, yf, k1, yf, skpo, k1, p30 [32, 35].
Row 6 As row 2.
Row 7 K31 [33, 36], yf, skpo, k2, yf, k1, sk2p, k1, yf, k3, yf, skpo, k2, yf, k1, sk2p, k1, yf, k2, k2tog, yf, k31 [33, 36].
Row 8 Purl.
Row 9 K32 [34, 37], (yf, sk2p, yf, k1) 6 times, k32 [34, 37].
Row 10 Purl.
These 10 rows form the pattern.
Rep these 10 rows 3 times more.
With RS facing and keeping patt as set:
Cast off 6 sts at beg of next 2 rows, then k2tog at beg of every row until 37 [41, 47] sts rem.
Cont in patt on these sts until 8 patts have been worked.
Now k2tog at each end of every row until 21 [25, 27] sts rem.
Cast off.

NECKBAND

Join shoulder seams. With RS facing and commencing at base of straight side of neck, rejoin yarn and, using 2.25mm needles, pick up and k 37 sts up right side of neck to shaping; pick up and k 34 sts along shaped edge; k across 34 [34, 38] sts on spare needle; pick up and k 34 sts along shaped edge and 37 sts down straight side. *(176 [176, 180] sts.)*
Work 7 rows in st st commencing with a p row.
Row 8 K1, *yf, k2tog. Rep from * to last st, k1.
Work 7 rows in st st commencing with a p row. Cast off.

SLEEVE BANDS

Join left shoulder seam. With RS facing, rejoin yarn and, using 2.25mm needles, pick up and k 76 [78, 82] sts evenly along lower edge of sleeve.
Work 7 rows in st st commencing with a p row.
Row 8 K1, *yf, k2tog. Rep from * to last st, k1.
Work 7 rows in st st commencing with a p row. Cast off.

FINISHING

Block or press carefully, as given on page 137.
Join side and sleeve seams.
Sew in sleeves, with centre of head of sleeve to shoulder seam.
Turn neckband and sleeve bands to WS at row of holes and sew down. Stitch each end of neckband to cast-off 8 sts at centre.
Sew hook and eye to front opening at start of neck shaping.

This fresh, zingy lime-green colour is the essence of summer, and the sleeveless top is knitted in a lovely mohair mix that is light as a feather. The armholes are trimmed with a pretty picot edge that finishes them off to perfection. Wear it with a full, brightly coloured printed skirt and it will see you through the day looking chic. This timeless simple top is easy to knit and easy to wear; it was designed by Rita for the modern woman who loves a retro look.

Doris Shell Top

Materials

YARN
5 [6, 7] x 25g balls Bergere de France Angel (44% polyamide, 32% acrylic, 24% mohair, approximately 275m/300 yards), shade 212.511 Granny

NEEDLES
1 pair needles size 3.75mm
1 pair needles size 4.5mm
Stitch holders

MEASUREMENTS
To fit Small [Medium, Large]
Actual chest size 84 [96, 104]cm
33 [37¾, 41]in
Length to back neck 48 [50, 52]cm
19 [19¾, 20½]in

TENSION
24 stitches and 28 rows measure 10cm/4in over pattern on 4.5mm needles (or size needed to obtain given tension)

Note: Use the yarn double throughout.

BACK
Using 3.75mm needles and yarn double, cast on 101 [117, 125] sts and work 5cm/2in in k1, p1 rib.
Change to 4.5mm needles and commence patt:
Row 1 K3, *yf, k2, p3tog, k2, yf, k1; rep from * to last 2 sts, k2.
Row 2 Purl.
Rep rows 1 and 2 twice more.
Row 7 K2, p2tog, *k2, yf, k1, yf, k2, p3tog; rep from * ending k2, yf, k1, yf, k2, p2tog, k2.
Row 8 Purl.
Rep rows 7 and 8 twice more.
These 12 rows form the pattern.
Cont in patt until work measures approximately 30 [32, 33]cm/12 [12½, 13]in, end on patt row 5 or 11.

SHAPE ARMHOLES
Cast on 8 sts at beg of next 2 rows.
Cont in patt until work measures 48 [50, 52]cm/ 19 [19¾, 20½]in, ending on patt row 5 or 11.
Next row P37 [45, 45], place marker, (k1, p1) 21 [21, 25] times, k1, place 2nd marker; patt to end.
Cont in patt but working sts between markers in moss st. Work until back measures 48 [50, 52]cm/19 [19¾, 20½]in, ending after a p row.
Next row K37 [45, 45], work 7 sts in moss st, cast off 29 [29, 37] sts, work 7 sts in moss st, patt to end.
Leave the 2 rem sets of sts on holders for shoulders.

FRONT

Work as for back to armhole shaping.

Shape armholes as for back, then work 17 rows in patt.

Next row P37 [45, 45], place marker, (k1, p1) 21 [21, 25] times, k1, place 2nd marker; patt to end.

Cont in patt as set for 6 more rows.

Next row Patt 37, work 7 sts in moss st, cast off 29 [29, 37] sts, work 7 sts in moss st, patt to end.

Work straight on sts for right front keeping 7 sts at neck edge in moss st.

When work measures same length as back, place shoulder sts of right front together with those of right back, with RS facing, and cast them off together.

Rejoin yarn at neck edge and work left front to match, reversing shaping.

Join left shoulder seam in the same way.

ARMHOLE EDGINGS

Using 3.75mm needles, pick up and k 84 [91, 98] sts along armhole edge.

Knit 1 row then work picot cast-off as follows:

Cast off 2 sts, *return rem st to LH needle and cast on 2 sts, cast off 4 sts. Rep from * to end, cast off any rem sts.

FINISHING

Do not block or press. Sew up side and underarm seams.

Alpaca yarn is used here, as it drapes beautifully on the neckline of this pretty lacy top. The early 1950s style is very easy to knit, and the alpaca makes a light, soft fabric. The rich yellow is the perfect summer colour and teams with black, white or any vibrant hue and print. Each side of the front neckline has a thread running through the stitches on the wrong side, which gives a gathered effect to the neck (see the detail photograph on page 30); these threads can be adjusted to be as tight or as loose as you wish.

Shirley Lace Top

Materials

YARN
5 x 50g balls Artesano 4ply 100% Superfine Alpaca (100% superfine alpaca, approximately 184m/ 204 yards), shade 8774 Ecuador

NEEDLES
1 pair needles size 2.25mm
1 pair needles size 3.25mm
1 crochet hook size 2.5mm

SPECIAL ABBREVIATION
sk2p slip 1, knit 2 together, pass slipped stitch over

MEASUREMENTS
Small [Medium, Large]
Actual chest size 80 [85, 88]cm
32 [38, 41]in
Length to back neck 53 [58, 63]cm
21 [22¾, 24¾]in

TENSION
30 stitches and 32 rows measure 10cm/4in over pattern on 3.25mm needles (or size needed to obtain given tension)

BACK
Using 2.25mm needles, cast on 108 [120, 132] sts.
Work 9cm/3½in in k1, p1 rib, inc 1 st at end of last row. (109 [121, 133] sts.)
Change to 3.25mm needles and pattern as follows:
Row 1 K1, (yf, skpo, k7, k2tog, yf, k1) to end.
Row 2 and every alt row Purl.
Row 3 K1, (yf, k1, skpo, k5, k2tog, k1, yf, k1) to end.
Row 5 K1, (yf, k2, skpo, k3, k2tog, k2, yf, k1) to end.
Row 7 K1, (yf, k3, skpo, k1, k2tog, k3, yf, k1) to end.
Row 9 K1, (yf, k4, sk2p, k4, yf, k1) to end.
Row 11 K1, (k3, k2tog, yf, k1, yf, skpo, k4) to end.
Row 13 K1, (k2, k2tog, k1, yf, k1, yf, k1, skpo, k3) to end.
Row 15 K1, (k1, k2tog, k2, yf, k1, yf, k2, skpo, k2) to end.
Row 17 K1, (k2tog, k3, yf, k1, yf, k3, skpo, k1) to end.
Row 19 Skpo, (k4, yf, k1, yf, k4, sk2p) to end, but finishing last rep skpo.
Row 20 Purl.
These 20 rows form the pattern.
Cont in patt, inc at both ends of next and every 6th foll row until there are 133 [145, 157] sts.
Cont until work measures 29 [32, 35]cm/11½ [12½, 13¾]in. Mark this point for the armholes.
Cont until work measures 47 [52, 57]cm/18½ [20½, 22½]in.

SHAPE SHOULDERS
Cast off 9 [10, 11] sts at beg of next 8 rows, then 10 [12, 13] sts at beg of next 2 rows.
Cast off 41 [41, 45] sts.

FRONT

Work as for back until armhole marker.

Cont until a 10th row of patt has been worked.

Divide sts for neck as follows:

Work 67 [73, 79] sts, turn.

Cont on this set of sts for the LS of neck until work measures 42cm/16½in with RS facing.

Work in patt to the last 24 sts, then k2tog 12 times.

Cont on these 55 [61, 67] sts, keeping patt as set at sleeve edge, until work corresponds to back to outer shoulder.

SHAPE SHOULDERS

Cast off 9 [10, 11] sts at shoulder edge on the next 3 alt rows. Working on rem 28 [31, 34] sts, keep neck edge straight and dec at shoulder edge on every row until all sts are worked off.

To complete right front, pick up the centre st (that is, the 67th [73rd, 79th] st which was worked for left front) and place it on LH needle, making 67 [73, 79] sts.

Complete to match left front, reversing shapings.

FINISHING

Block or press carefully, as given on page 137.

Join side seams; join shoulder seams.

Using crochet hook, work a row of dc around neck and armholes and finish with edging as follows (see page 139): *3ch, 1dc into first of these ch, 1dc into dc of previous row. Rep from * all around.

Where the 12 decreases were made on the fronts, run a strand of yarn along the WS of the row to gather them up; fasten strand at each end when desired gathers are made (see detail above).

This pretty knitted blouse, with its openwork stitch and detail around the neck, is a pattern straight from the late 1940s. Then, it would have added a feminine touch to sharp tailoring, and it would set off many modern outfits as well as in its original heyday. The luxurious cashmere and merino yarn feels beautiful next to the skin and keeps off the chill on cooler summer days. The buttons at the back of the neck are a lovely vintage detail.

Louise Latticework Jersey

Materials

YARN

6 [7, 8] x 50g balls Sublime Baby Cashmere Merino Silk 4ply (75% extra fine merino wool, 20% silk, 5% cashmere, approximately 170m/ 184 yards), shade 05 Waterlily

NEEDLES

1 pair needles size 3mm
1 pair needles size 3.75mm
1 crochet hook size 3mm

NOTIONS

6 buttons, 1.5cm/⅝in in diameter

SPECIAL ABBREVIATION

cross p2tog sl next st off LH needle and leave at front of work, sl next st onto RH needle, using LH needle pick up first st, then place 2nd st back onto LH needle, p these 2 sts tog

MEASUREMENTS

To fit Small [Medium, Large]
Actual chest size 87 [93, 97]cm/34¼ [36½, 38]in
Length to back neck 47 [49, 51]cm/18½ [19, 20]in
Underarm sleeve 16cm/6in all sizes

TENSION

32 stitches and 30 rows measure 10cm/4in over pattern on 3.75mm needles (or size needed to obtain given tension)

BACK

Using 3mm needles, cast on 98 [114, 130] sts.
Next row Sl1, k to end of row.
Rep this row 5 times.
Work in patt as follows:
Row 1 Sl1, k1, *p2, k2tog, yf, k2, yf, skpo, p2, k2, rep from * to end of row.
Row 2 Sl1, *p1, k1, p2tog, yf, k1, p2, k1, yrn, p2tog, k1, p1, rep from * to last st, k1.
Row 3 Sl1, k1, *k2tog, yrn, p2, k2, p2, yf, skpo, k2, rep from * to end.
Row 4 Sl1, *p2tog, yf, k3, p2, k3, yrn, cross p2tog, rep from * to last st, k1.
Row 5 Sl1, k1, *yf, skpo, p2, k2, p2, k2tog, yf, k2, rep from * to end.
Row 6 Sl1, *p1, k1, yrn, p2tog, k1, p2, k1, p2tog, yf, k1, p1, rep from * to last st, k1.
Row 7 Sl1, k1, *p2, yf, skpo, k2, k2tog, yrn, p2, rep from * to end.
Row 8 Sl1, *p1, k3, yrn, cross p2tog, p2tog, yf, k3, p1, rep from * to last st, k1.
These 8 rows form the pattern.
Rep these 8 rows 3 times more.
Change to size 3.75mm needles. Rep the 8 patt rows once. Keeping cont of patt, inc 1 st at each end of next and every foll 6th row until there are 122 [138, 154] sts on needle.
Cont without shaping until work measures 33 [35, 37]cm/ 13 [14, 14½]in from beg, ending with row 8 of patt.

SHAPE ARMHOLES

Cast off 7 sts at beg of next 2 rows. Keeping cont of patt, dec once at each end of every foll row until 98 [112, 126] sts rem. Work 1 row without shaping.

BACK OPENING

Next row Sl1, k1, (p2, k2tog, yf, k2, yf, skpo, p2, k2)
4 [4, 5] times, k to end, turn. Cont in patt on these
50 [58, 64] sts until 22 patts have been worked from beg.

SHAPE NECK AND SHOULDER

Row 1 Cast off 7 sts, work in patt to end of row.
Row 2 Work in patt to last 2 sts, k2tog.
Row 3 Cast off 3 sts, work in patt to end of row.
Row 4 Cast off 6 sts, work in patt to last 2 sts, k2tog.
Row 5 Cast off 3 sts, work in patt to end of row.
Rep rows 4 and 5 twice more. Cast off rem sts.
Return to sts left on needle. Rejoin yarn and cast on 2 sts
for underlay. Work to match first side, reversing shapings.

BACK NECK BORDERS

Using 3mm needles and with RS facing, pick up and k 32 [36,
40] sts along neck edge from right shoulder to back opening.
Work 6 rows in g st. Cast off.
Work LS of back to correspond by picking up 32 [36, 40] sts
along neck edge from back opening to left shoulder and working
6 rows in g st.

FRONT

Using 3mm needles, cast on 98 [114, 130] sts.
Work as given for back until armhole shapings are complete
and there are 98 [112, 126] sts on needle.
Cont in patt without shaping until work measures 40.5 [42,
44]cm/16 [16½, 17½]in from beg, ending with row 8 of patt.

YOKE

Row 1 Sl1, p to last st, k1.
Row 2 Sl1, k45 [49, 55], cast off 6 [7, 7] sts, k46 [50, 56].
Working across last 46 [50, 56] sts only, proceed as follows:
Row 3 Sl1, p to last 2 sts, k2tog.
Row 4 Cast off 2 sts, k to end of row.
Rep rows 3 and 4 four times more. *(31 [35, 41] sts.)*
Row 13 Sl1, p to last 2 sts, k2tog.
Row 14 K2tog, k to end of row.
Rep rows 13 and 14 five [5, 6] times more, then row
13 once. *(18 [22, 26] sts.)*
Next row Sl1, k to end of row.
Work 2 rows in reverse st st (1 row p, 1 row k).

SHAPE SHOULDER

Row 1 Cast off 9 [11, 13] sts, p to last st, k1.
Row 2 Sl1, k to end of row.
Turn and cast off 9 [11, 13] rem sts.
Rejoin yarn to inside edge of rem sts, and work as for first
section, reversing shapings.

FRONT NECK BORDERS

Using 3.75mm needles and with RS facing, pick up and k 87
[95, 103] sts evenly around neck edge. Work 6 rows in g st.
Small: Next row Sl1, *k2tog, k5, rep from * to last 2 sts, k2. *(74 sts.)*
Medium: Next row Sl1, k6, k2tog, *k8, k2tog, rep from *
to last 6 sts, k6. *(86 sts.)*
Large: Next row Sl1, k9, k2tog, *k12, k2tog, rep from *
to last 8 sts, k8. *(96 sts.)*
Rep rows 1–8 of patt, as given at beg of back, once.
Change to 3mm needles. Work 6 rows in g st. Cast off.

SLEEVES

Using 3mm needles, cast on 74 [86, 86] sts.
Row 1 Sl1, k to end of row. Rep this row 5 times.
Rep rows 1–8 of patt, as given at beg of back, once.
Change to 3.75mm needles. Keeping cont of patt, inc 1 st
at each end of next and every foll 4th row until there are 90
[102, 102] sts on needle. If there are not enough sts to form a
complete patt, work them in st st. Cont without shaping until
work measures 13cm/5in from beg, ending on WS.

SHAPE TOP OF SLEEVE

Cast off 2 sts at beg of every row until 74 [86, 86] sts rem.
Dec 1 st at beg of every row until 30 sts rem. Cast off 6 sts at
beg of next 4 rows. Cast off rem sts. Work a second sleeve.

FINISHING

Block or press carefully, as given on page 137. Sew up side,
shoulder and sleeve seams. Sew in sleeves, placing seam
to seam. Sew underlay in position on WS. Using crochet
hook, work 1 row of dc along each side of back opening (see
page 139). Crochet 6 small button loops down RH side of
opening. Sew on buttons to match buttonholes.

This beautiful plunge-neck top is as stylish today as it was on the 'sweater girls' of the 1950s. The retro chevron pattern is very flattering and definitely a look worth reviving. Knitted in an unusual bamboo yarn in a gorgeous pale pink shade, this top will be both cool and good looking in the summer. Great with a tan, it is the perfect holiday sweater to go with all your summer skirts and trousers.

Marilyn Magyar Top

Materials

YARN
9 x 50g balls Bergere de France Origin Bambou (100% bamboo viscose, approximately 80m/ 87.5 yards), shade 211 Equilibre

NEEDLES
I pair needles size 2.75mm
I pair needles size 3mm

SPECIAL ABBREVIATION
ssk slip I, slip I, as if to knit, insert LH needle into front of these 2 sts from L to R, then knit together

MEASUREMENTS
To fit sizes Small [Medium, Large]
Actual chest size 93 [99, 104]cm
37 [39, 41]in
Length to back neck 55 [58, 61]cm
21½ [22¾, 24]in

TENSION
26 stitches and 36 rows measure 10cm/4in over pattern on 3mm needles (or size needed to obtain given tension)

FRONT
Using 2.75mm needles, cast on 89 [105, 119] sts.
Row I K2, *pI, kI, rep from * to last st, kI.
Row 2 KI, *pI, kI, rep from * to end of row.
Rep these 2 rows until ribbing measures 9 [9, 9.5]cm/ 3½ [3½, 3¾]in from beg, ending with row I.

Change to 3mm needles and cont as follows:
Row I K6, (k2tog, yf, k5) 5 [6, 7] times, k2tog, yf, kI, pI, kI, yf, ssk, (k5, yf, ssk) 5 [6, 7] times, k6.
Row 2 and all alt rows KI, p43 [51, 58], kI, p43 [51, 58], kI.
Row 3 K5, (k2tog, yf, k5) 5 [6, 7] times, k2tog, yf, k2, pI, k2, yf, ssk, (k5, yf, ssk) 5 [6, 7] times, k5.
Row 5 K4, (k2tog, yf, k5) 5 [6, 7] times, k2tog, yf, k3, pI, k3, yf, ssk, (k5, yf, ssk) 5 [6, 7] times, k4.
Row 7 K3, (k2tog, yf, k5) 5 [6, 7] times, k2tog, yf, k4, pI, k4, yf, ssk, (k5, yf, ssk) 5 [6, 7] times, k3.
Row 9 K2, (k2tog, yf, k5) 5 [6, 7] times, k2tog, yf, k5, pI, k5, yf, ssk, (k5, yf, ssk) 5 [6, 7] times, k2.
Row II KI, (k2tog, yf, k5) 5 [6, 7] times, k2tog, yf, k6, pI, k6, yf, ssk, (k5, yf, ssk) 5 [6, 7] times, kI.
Row 13 (K2tog, yf, k5) 5 [6, 7] times, k2tog, yf, k7, pI, k7, yf, ssk, (k5, yf, ssk) 5 [6, 7] times.
Row 14 As row 2.
These 14 rows form the pattern.

COMMENCE SIDE SHAPING
Row 15 KI, mI, k5, (k2tog, yf, k5) 5 [6, 7] times, k2tog, yf, kI, pI, kI, yf, ssk, (k5, yf, ssk) 5 [6, 7] times, k4, mI, k2.
Row 16 (KI, p44 [52, 59]) twice, kI.
Row 17 K6, (k2tog, yf, k5) 5 [6, 7] times, k2tog, yf, k2, pI, k2, yf, ssk, (k5, yf, ssk), 5 [6, 7] times, k6.
Row 18 As row 16.

Row 19 K5, (k2tog, yf, k5) 5 [6, 7] times, k2tog, yf, k3, p1, k3, yf, ssk, (k5, yf, ssk) 5 [6, 7] times, k5.
Row 20 As row 16.
Cont in patt, inc 1 st at each end of row, keeping inc sts in patt, in next and every foll 6th row until there are 117 [133, 147] sts on needle.
Work 2 [6, 8] rows in patt, ending with an odd numbered row.**

SHAPE NECK AND SLEEVE
Next row Cast on 2 sts, work 60 [68, 75] sts, cast off 1 st (centre st), work 58 [66, 73], cast on 2 sts.
Cont on last 60 [68, 75] sts as follows:
Row 1 Work in patt to last 3 sts, k2tog, k1.
Row 2 K1, p to end of row, cast on 2 sts.
Rep rows 1 and 2 four times. (65 [73, 80] sts.)

Keeping armhole edge straight, cont dec at neck edge in next and every alt row until 36 [42, 49] sts rem. Work 3 [5, 7] rows without shaping, ending with a p row.

SHAPE SHOULDER
Row 1 Cast off 12 [14, 17] sts, work in patt to end.
Row 2 K1, p to end.
Row 3 Cast off 6 [7, 8] sts, work in patt to end.
Row 4 K1, p to end.
Rep rows 3 and 4 twice more. Cast off rem 6 [7, 8] sts.
Rejoin yarn at neck edge of rem sts. Work to match first side, reversing shapings.

BACK
Work as given for front to **.
Work 12 rows in patt, casting on 2 sts at beg of every row. *(141 [157, 171] sts.)*
Cont in patt without shaping until armhole measures 7 rows less than front armhole, ending with a patt row.

SHAPE NECK
Next row K1, p41 [47, 54], cast off 57 sts fairly loosely, p41 [47, 54], k1.
Work 6 rows in patt on last 42 [48, 55] sts, dec 1 st at neck edge in every row.
Shape shoulder as given for front.
Rejoin yarn at neck edge of rem 42 [48, 55] sts, and work to match first side, reversing shapings.

SLEEVE BANDS
Using 2.75mm needles, cast on 9 [10, 10] sts and work every row knit, firmly and evenly, until band measures 30 [32, 34]cm/12 [12½, 13]in unstretched.
Cast off evenly k-wise.
Work a second sleeve band in the same way.

NECKBAND
Using 2.75mm needles, cast on 10 [10, 11] sts and work every row knit, firmly and evenly, until band measures 82 [86, 90]cm/32 [34, 35]in unstretched.
Cast off evenly k-wise.

FINISHING
Block or press carefully, as given on page 137, stretching plain knitted bands slightly.
Sew shoulder seams, sew up side seams, including sleeve extensions.
Join short sides of bands and sew evenly around armhole and neck edges, crossing the neckband at centre front, as illustrated.

This original design was created by Rita specially for the book, inspired by the popular fashions of the 1950s but with an undeniable up-to-date appeal. The contrast crochet edging makes an attractive finish that is a true vintage detail. The mercerized cotton and lacy stitch are cool and neat, combining to make a top that is easy to wear as well as being reminiscent of the pretty cotton tops of yesterday. Wear it with chic Capri pants or a dramatic full skirt for maximum effect.

Kate Lace-Panel Blouse

Materials

YARN

Wendy Supreme Luxury Cotton 4ply (100% mercerized cotton, approximately 239m/ 219 yards):
3 x 100g balls, shade 1833 Black
1 x 100g ball, shade 1851 Cream

NEEDLES

1 pair needles size 3.25mm
1 crochet hook size 2.5mm
Stitch holders

NOTIONS

6 small buttons of choice (optional)

MEASUREMENTS

To fit Small [Medium, Large]
Actual chest size 81 [92, 102]cm
32 [36½, 40]in
Length to back neck 48 [54, 57]cm
19 [21¼, 22½]in
Underarm sleeve 8 [10, 12]cm
3 [4, 5]in

TENSION

23 stitches and 30 rows measure 10cm/4in over pattern on 3.25mm needles (or size needed to obtain given tension)

BACK

Using 3.25mm needles and black yarn, cast on 96 [104, 112] sts and knit 1 row.
Cont in patt as follows:
Row 1 P2, (yon, p4tog) to last 2, p2.
Row 2 K3, (k1, p1, k1) into next st, *k1, (k1, p1, k1) into next st, rep from * to last 2 sts, k2.
Row 3 Knit.
These 3 rows form the pattern.
Rep these 3 rows until work measures 12 [15, 15]cm/ 4¾ [6, 6]in.
Work 6cm/2¼in in k1, p1 rib for waist.
Change back to lace patt and cont until work measures 32 [34, 37]cm/12½ [13¼, 14½]in.

SHAPE ARMHOLE

Cast off 5 [5, 6] sts at beg of next 2 rows.
Dec 1 st at each end of every alt row until 76 [82, 86] sts rem.
Cont until armhole measures 20cm/8in.

SHAPE SHOULDER

Cast off 8 [8, 9] sts at beg of next 2 rows and 8 [9, 9] sts at beg of foll 2 rows; 45 [48, 50] sts rem for back of neck.
Cast off loosely.

FRONT

Using 3.25mm needles and black yarn, cast on 97 [105, 113] sts and knit 1 row.
Patt 40 [44, 48] sts, (p1, k1) 8 times, p1, patt 40 [44, 48] sts.
Cont as set with centre 17 sts in st st until armhole measures 3cm/1in with 77 [83, 87] sts rem.

SHAPE NECK

Work 31 [33, 36] sts and place on stitch holder.

Cast off next 15 sts in rib.

Work rem 31 [33, 36] sts.

Cont armhole shaping until 12 rows have been worked from beg of armhole, AT THE SAME TIME dec 1 st at neck edge every row 7 times, then dec 1 st at neck edge every alt row, until 16 [17, 18] sts rem.

Cont until armhole measures 20cm/8in.

SHAPE SHOULDER

Cast off 8 [8, 9] sts at beg of next row and 8 [9, 9] sts at beg of foll alt row.

Return to 31 [33, 36] sts on stitch holder and work other side of neck to match.

SLEEVES

Using 3.25mm needles and black yarn, cast on 64 [68, 72] sts and knit 1 row.

Cont in patt, inc 1 st at each end of 5th row, then every 4th row to 72 [76, 80] sts.

Keeping patt as set, work until sleeve measures 8 [10, 12]cm/ 3 [4, 4¾]in.

SHAPE TOP OF SLEEVE

Cast off 5 [6, 6] sts at beg of next 2 rows.

Dec 1 st at each end of every row 0 [3, 1] times; then every alt row 20 [16, 21] times; then every row 0 [3, 1] times.

Cast off rem 22 [22, 24] sts.

Work a second sleeve in the same way.

SHOULDER SEAMS

Sew front to back along shoulder seams.

FINISHING

Block or press carefully, as given on page 137.

Sew sleeve top to armhole, easing to fit.

Sew side and sleeve seams.

Using cream yarn and crochet hook, work 1 row dc along outer edge of centre rib panel, working into every k st.

Turn, *3ch, miss 2dc, 1dc into next st; rep from * to end.

Fasten off. (See page 139.)

Work 3 more of these trims on the centre panel, first on the other outside edge and then on 3rd knit sts in from each side.

Work the same trim around the neck and sleeve edges.

Sew in all loose ends.

Sew buttons to front of blouse as illustrated.

Cute Cardigans

The 7th Earl of Cardigan is said to be the originator of the cardigan, having reportedly worn one during the Crimean War in the mid-nineteenth century. Whether the idea came from adding sleeves to a waistcoat or buttons to a sweater, no one seems to know. The cardigan has taken many forms, from thick and cosy to light and lacy, from casual and loose to formal and fitted. Knitted in many different fibres – cotton, silk, cashmere, mohair or angora – it has proved to be a versatile and much-loved garment for men and women. In the course of its fashion history the cardigan has been designed to be worn closed as a sweater or open with something underneath. When paired with a matching fitted sweater it is known as a twinset (see page 94). The cardigans here are typical of the 1930s, 1940s and 1950s. You can trace the different lines dictated by fashion from the extravagantly pleated *Wallis* Cardigan (see page 60), via the prettily patterned Tyrolean style of the 1940s (see page 46), to the much-loved and glamorous bolero so typical of the 1950s (see page 52).

This Tyrolean cardigan with Fair Isle panels has the essence of 1940s fashion. The contrast stars would have been worked in any oddments of yarn, but we have designed a pretty colourway in greens with pink and lilac in keeping with the period look. The pattern is worked from a chart and requires a degree of knitting skill (see pages 135–6).

Hedy Tyrolean-Pattern Cardigan

Materials

YARN
Sublime Baby Cashmere Merino Silk 4ply
(75% extra fine merino, 20% silk, 5% cashmere, approximately 170m/184 yards):
7 [8, 9] x 50g balls, shade 04 Gooseberry (A)
1 x 50g ball, shade 206 Little Pinkie (B)
1 x 50g ball, shade 205 Sweet Pea (C)

Sublime Extra Fine Merino Wool 4ply (100% extra fine merino wool, approximately 175m/191 yards):
1 x 50g ball, shade 288 Sateen (D)
1 x 50g ball, shade 08 Grosgrain (E)

NEEDLES
1 pair needles size 2.75mm
1 pair needles size 3.25mm
Stitch holders
Safety pins

NOTIONS
11 [11, 12] buttons, 2cm/¾in in diameter

MEASUREMENTS
To fit Small [Medium, Large]
Actual chest size 81 [89, 99]cm/32 [35, 37]in
Length to back neck 48 [49, 52]cm/19 [19¼, 20½]in
Underarm sleeve 20 [21, 22]cm/8 [8¼, 8½]in

TENSION
28 stitches and 36 rows measure 10cm/4in over pattern on 3.25mm needles (or size needed to obtain given tension)

RIGHT FRONT
Using 2.75mm needles and yarn A, cast on 44 [46, 52] sts. Work in k1, p1 rib for 8cm/3in.
Change to size 3.25mm needles and work 4 [4, 6] rows st st.
Next row Using yarn A, k7; then k25 across row 1 of chart; using yarn A, k to end. This row sets position of chart.

Cont working from chart as set until 4 stars have been completed, AT THE SAME TIME inc 1 st at outside edge of next row, then every foll 3rd row until there are 57 [60, 67] sts. When all stars are complete, work 2 rows st st then change to moss st for rest of yoke. Work straight until work measures 28 [28, 30]cm/11 [11, 12]in.

SHAPE ARMHOLE
Cast off 6 [7, 8] sts at armhole edge of next row and dec at same edge of alt rows until 40 [43, 46] sts rem.
Cont until armhole measures 12 [12, 13]cm/4¾ [4¾, 5]in.

SHAPE NECK
With WS facing, work 32 [36, 37] sts. Slip last 6 [7, 9] sts onto a stitch holder for the neckband.
Next row Dec 1 st at neck edge (right end) of every row until 24 [26, 26] sts rem.
Cont until armhole measures 19 [19, 20]cm/7½ [7½, 8]in.

SHAPE SHOULDER
Cast off 8 sts at beg of next 2 rows and 8 [9, 9] sts at same edge of foll 2 alt rows.

LEFT FRONT
Work as for right front to **.
Next row Using yarn A, k12 [14, 20], work 25 sts of chart, with yarn A, k7.
Cont as for right front, reversing shapings.

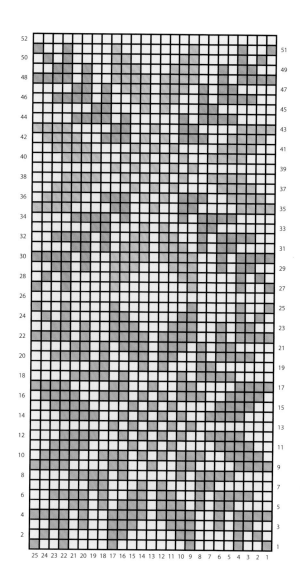

KEY

- ☐ A Gooseberry
- ▨ B Little Pinkie
- ▨ C Sweet Pea
- ▨ D Sateen
- ▨ E Grosgrain

BACK

Using 2.75mm needles and yarn A, cast on 105 [115, 121] sts and work in k1, p1 rib for 8cm/3in as for fronts, ending with row 2.

Change to 3.25mm needles and work 4 rows in st st.

Inc 1 st at each end of next row, then every foll 3rd row to 119 [127, 141] sts.

Work straight until work measures 28 [29, 30]cm/ 11 [11½, 12]in.

When st st section measures same as fronts, cont in moss st.

Row 1 P1, (k1, p1) to last st, k1.

Row 2 K1, (p1, k1) to last st, p1.

SHAPE ARMHOLE

Cast off 7 [7, 8] sts at beg of next 2 rows.

Dec 1 st at each end of every alt row until 89 [93, 99] sts rem.

Work until armhole measures 19 [19, 20]cm/7½ [7½, 8]in.

SHAPE SHOULDER

Cast off 8 sts at beg of next 4 [2, 2] rows.

Cast off 8 [9, 9] sts at beg of foll 2 [4, 4] rows.

41 [41, 47] sts rem for back of neck.

Place sts on a stitch holder.

SLEEVES

Using 2.75mm needles and yarn A, cast on 65 [65, 71] sts and work 2.5cm/1in in rib as for fronts.

Change to size 3.25mm needles and st st.
Inc 1 st at each end of 7th row, then every foll 8th row,
until 79 [81, 87] sts rem.
Work straight until sleeve measures 20 [22, 22]cm/
8 [8½, 8½]in.

SHAPE TOP OF SLEEVE
Cast off 7 [7, 8] sts at beg of next 2 rows. (63 [67, 71] sts.)
Dec 1 st at each end of every 2nd row 8 [7, 7] times, then
dec 1 st at each end of every 3rd row 6 [8, 8] times, then
dec 1 st at each end of every 2nd row 7 [6, 7] times.
Cast off rem sts loosely.

Work a second sleeve in the same way.
Join shoulder seams.

LEFT BAND
Using 2.75mm needles and yarn A, cast on 11 sts and work
rib as for back welt until band is long enough when slightly
stretched to fit front edge. Break yarn and leave sts on
safety pin.

RIGHT BAND
Using 2.75mm needles and yarn A, cast on 11 sts and work 8
[10, 6] rows in k1, p1 rib, then make a buttonhole (see page 137).
Buttonhole row 1 Rib 4, cast off 2, then rib to end.
Buttonhole row 2 Rib to last 4 sts, cast on 2, rib 4.
Work 12 [12, 10] rows rib then rep these 2 rows.
Rep from * to * 9 [9, 10] times. Then rib 6 [8, 6] rows.
Break off yarn and leave sts on another safety pin.
Now work neck ribbing as follows:
With RS facing, join yarn A and, using 2.75mm needles,
rib 11 sts from safety pin at right front band, then k 6
[7, 9] sts from holder, pick up and k 30 [32, 32] sts along
RS of neck edge up to shoulder seam, k 41 [41, 47] across
sts on stitch holder (back neck), then pick up and k 30
[32, 32] sts along left neck edge, k 6 [7, 9] sts from holder,
then rib 11 sts on safety pin at left front band. Work 8 rows
rib, making a buttonhole as in band on 4th and 5th rows
at right front edge. Cast off.

FINISHING
Block or press carefully, as given on page 137. Set in sleeves,
then sew up side and sleeve seams. Sew bands neatly to front
edges. Sew on buttons to match buttonholes.

This angora bolero is early 1950s glamour personified. It is knitted in soft, pure angora, and the band is given extra sparkle by the addition of small beads. We chose a soft silver grey, but this yarn comes in a beautiful range of colours. The bolero could be worn over a stunning evening gown or it could dress up a simple top for a night on the town. It has all the hallmarks of Hollywood and, wearing it, you will feel like a movie star.

Ava Angora Bolero

Materials

YARN
4 x 50g balls Orkney Angora Incredible Angora 4ply (100% angora, approximately 400m/ 437 yards), shade 29 Silver

NEEDLES
I pair needles size 3.75mm
I pair needles size 5mm
I circular needle size 3.75mm
Stitch holder

NOTIONS
470 [494, 518] 6mm/¼in beads

SPECIAL ABBREVIATION
bead1 move bead close to tip of needle then slip next stitch purlwise (see page 137)

MEASUREMENTS
To fit Small [Medium, Large]
Actual chest size 86 [91, 97]cm
34 [36, 38]in
Length to back neck 37 [41, 45]cm
14½ [16, 17¾]in
Underarm sleeve 11cm/4½in all sizes

TENSION
20 stitches and 26 rows measure 10cm/4in over stocking stitch on 5mm needles (or size needed to obtain given tension) using the yarn double

Note: Use the yarn double throughout.

LEFT FRONT
Using 5mm needles and yarn double, cast on 17 sts and k 1 row.
Cont in st st and shape front edge by casting on 3 sts at beg of next and alt rows 3 times altogether. *(26 [29, 32] sts.)*
Cast on 2 sts at beg of next and alt rows 3 times. *(32 [35, 38] sts.)*
Row 11 Knit.
Row 12 Inc in first st, p to last st, inc in last st.
Row 13 Knit.
Row 14 Inc in first st, p to end.
Rep last 4 rows once. This completes front shaping.
Cont in st st, inc at side edge on every 4th row until 3 more incs have been worked. *(38 [41, 44] sts.)*
Cont straight until side edge measures 15 [18, 21]cm/ 6 [7, 8¼]in, ending with a p row.

SHAPE ARMHOLE
Cast off 4 sts at beg of next row, then dec 1 st at same edge on every row until 28 [31, 34] sts rem.
Cont straight until work measures 23 [26, 29]cm/ 9 [10, 11½]in ending at front edge.

SHAPE FRONT
Dec 1 st at front edge on next and every foll 12th row 3 times. Cont straight until work measures 36 [40, 44]cm/ 14 [15¾, 17]in, ending at armhole edge.

SHAPE SHOULDER
Cast off 8 [9, 10] sts at armhole edge on alt rows twice.
Cast off rem sts.

RIGHT FRONT

Work to match left front, but reverse shapings by beg with a purl row instead of a knit row and substitute p for k and k for p throughout.

BACK

Using 5mm needles, cast on 80 [90, 100] sts and work 11 rows in st st. Cont in st st, inc 1 st at both ends of next and every foll 4th row until there are 90 [100, 110] sts. Cont straight until work measures 15 [18, 21]cm/6 [7, 8¼]in.

SHAPE ARMHOLES

Cast off 4 sts at beg of next 2 rows, then dec 1 st at both ends of every row until 70 [76, 82] sts rem. Cont straight until work measures 36 [40, 44]cm/14 [15¾, 17]in.

SHAPE SHOULDERS

Cast off 8 [9, 10] sts at beg of next 4 rows, then 9 [10, 10] sts at beg of foll 2 rows. Leave rem sts for neckband on holder.

SLEEVES

Thread 41 [43, 45] beads onto double yarn. Using 3.75mm needles, cast on 55 [59, 63] sts and work 2 rows in k1, p1 rib.
Row 3 K1, p1, k1 (bead1, k1, p1, k1) to end.
Row 4 K1, p1 rib as set.
Row 5 K1, (bead1, k1, p1, k1) to last 2 sts, k1, p1.
Row 6 As row 4.
Row 7 As row 3.
Row 8 As row 4.
Change to 5mm needles, inc 1 st at beg of next row and cont in st st, inc 1 st at both ends of 5th and every foll 4th row until there are 66 [72, 78] sts. Cont straight until work measures 11cm/4½in.

SHAPE TOP OF SLEEVE

Cast off 4 sts at beg of next 2 rows. Dec 1 st at both ends of alt rows until 60 [66, 72] sts rem, then dec 1 st at both ends of every row until 20 sts rem. Cast off 2 sts at beg of next 4 rows. Cast off. Work a second sleeve in the same way.

BORDERS

Thread 388 [408, 428] beads onto double yarn (see page 137). Using the 3.75mm circular needle, pick up and k a total of 388 [408, 428] sts all around edge, beginning at one of the side seams and knitting across sts on holder at back neck when you come to them (these sts are included in the stitch count). Work 2 rows k1, p1 rib. Work as on cuffs for 8 rows. Cast off.

FINISHING

Do not block or press. Join side, shoulder and sleeve seams. Sew in sleeves.

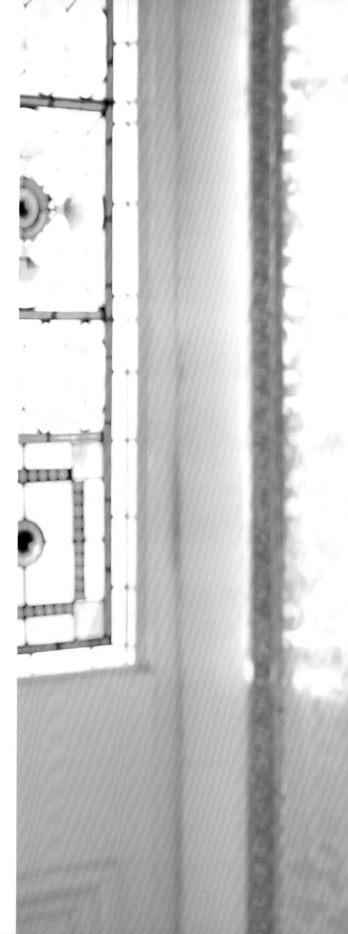

The prettiest lace cardigan comes straight from the late 1940s to your wardrobe. It is knitted in a soft merino wool in 3ply weight, which comes in a beautiful range of colours. This sugar pink is just right for the period, as are the flattering high waist and neat vintage buttons; the row of double crochet finishes it off to perfection.

Lauren Lace-Stitch Cardigan

Materials

YARN
5 x 50g balls Adriafil Avantgarde 3ply (100% superwash merino wool, approximately 220m/ 240 yards), shade 94 BonBon

NEEDLES
1 pair needles size 3mm
1 pair needles size 4mm
1 crochet hook size 3mm

NOTIONS
4 buttons, 1cm/½in in diameter

SPECIAL ABBREVIATION
ML make lace as follows: yf, insert needle into next 3 sts as if to p them tog, then p1, k1, p1 into these 3 sts, each time slipping the needle into them as if they were all 1 st, then yb, k1

MEASUREMENTS
To fit Small [Medium, Large]
Actual chest size 81 [86, 90]cm
32 [34, 35½]in
Length to back neck 54 [58, 61]cm
21 [23, 24]in
Underarm sleeve 11 [12, 14]cm
4 [5, 5½]in

TENSION
30 stitches and 36 rows rows measure 10cm/4in over pattern on 4mm needles (or size needed to obtain given tension)

BACK
Using 3mm needles, cast on 121 [135, 151] sts.
Row 1 (RS) P1, (k1, p1) to end.
Row 2 K1, (p1, k1) to end.
Rep these 2 rows 35 times more, but inc 1 st at each end of last row. *(123 [137, 153] sts.)*
Change to 4mm needles and commence patt as follows:
Row 1 K1, *ML, rep from * to last st, k1.
Row 2 Purl.
These 2 rows form the pattern. Rep these 2 rows until work measures 35 [37, 39]cm/14 [14½, 15]in.

SHAPE ARMHOLES
Note: When a dec breaks into a group of 3 sts in lace patt, the remainder of the 3 sts should be worked st st.
Keeping patt as set, cast off 8 sts at beg of next 2 rows, then dec 1 st at each end of foll 4 [6, 8] rows.
Dec 1 st at beg of next 8 [10, 12] rows. *(91 [99, 109] sts.)*
Rep the 2 pattern rows until armholes measure 18 [19.5, 21]cm/ 7 [7½, 8]in.

SHAPE SHOULDERS
Cast off 8 [10, 12] sts at beg of next 8 rows.
Cast off rem sts for back neck.

LEFT FRONT
Using 3mm needles, cast on 61 [69, 77] sts. Work rib as for back.
Change to 4mm needles and work the 2 pattern rows once, then, keeping cont of patt, commence front shaping.
Dec 1 st at end of next row and every foll 8th row until 55 [63, 71] sts rem.
Work another 3 rows. Dec 1 st at front edge on next row.
Cont until work measures same as back to armhole.

SHAPE ARMHOLE

Cont to dec at front edge on every 4th row, work
as follows:
Next row Cast off 8 sts, then work in patt to end.
Next row Purl.
**Work 5 [5, 7] rows, dec 1 st at armhole edge on each
of these rows.
Work another 6 [10, 12] rows, dec 1 st at armhole edge
on alt rows. *(35 [45, 50] sts.)*
Cont to dec 1 st at front edge on every 4th row until
32 [40, 48] sts rem.**
Work 1 row straight.

SHAPE SHOULDER

Cast off 8 [10, 12] sts at beg of next 3 alt rows beg from
armhole end, then work 1 row. Cast off rem sts.

RIGHT FRONT

As left front, but make buttonholes after 6 rows of rib
as follows (see page 137):
Buttonhole row 1 Rib 5, cast off 3 sts, rib to end.
Buttonhole row 2 Work in rib, casting on 3 sts over
those cast off.
Work 18 rows in rib. Rep the last 20 rows twice more,
then work the 2 buttonhole rows again. Work 4 more
rows in rib.
Change to 4mm needles and complete as for left front,
reversing shapings.

SLEEVES

Using 3mm needles, cast on 77 [83, 89] sts and work the
2 rib rows given for the back 8 times.
Change to 4mm needles and work the 2 patt rows until
sleeve seam measures 11 [12, 14]cm/4 [5, 5½]in.

SHAPE TOP OF SLEEVE

Keeping cont of patt, cast off 8 sts at beg of next 2 rows,
then dec 1 st at beg of every row until 31 [39, 47] sts rem.
Cast off 4 sts at beg of next 6 rows. Cast off rem sts.
Work a second sleeve in the same way.

FINISHING

Using 3mm crochet hook, starting at bottom of right
front, work 1 row dc along front edge, around back
neck and down left front (see page 139). Fasten off.
Block or press carefully, as given on page 137.
Join shoulder seams and sew sleeves into armholes.
Sew up side and sleeve seams, and press seams lightly.
Sew on buttons to match buttonholes.

A cardigan is a must-have in any knitwear collection and this is a flattering shape from the late 1930s. When Wallis Simpson married the Duke of Windsor in 1937, she wore a jacket with a shape similar to this cardigan — very fitted but with a line of gathers under the bust and buttons down to the waist. Although harking back to a bygone era, this cardigan could be worn today with a multitude of styles, either over a tee-shirt or blouse or on its own, and the small roll collar is neat enough to sit under a coat.

Wallis Pleated Cardigan

Materials

YARN
10 x 50g balls Rowan Pure Wool 4ply (100% pure new wool, approximately 160m/174 yards), shade 450 Eau de Nil

NEEDLES
1 pair needles size 2.75mm
1 pair needles size 3.25mm
Stitch holder

NOTIONS
7 buttons, 2cm/¾in in diameter

MEASUREMENTS
One size
To fit bust 81–96.5cm/32–38in
Length to back neck 53cm/21in
Underarm sleeve 51cm/20in

Note: The sizing on this pattern is extremely flexible because of the pleated style

TENSION
28 stitches and 36 rows measure 10cm/4in over stocking stitch on size 3.25mm needles (or size needed to obtain given tension)

LEFT FRONT
Using 2.75mm needles, cast on 76 sts.
Row 1 *P2, k2, rep from * to end.
Row 2 As row 1.
Rep these 2 rows until work measures 13cm/5in.

SHAPE SIDE SEAM
With RS facing, inc 1 st at beg of next and every 6th row.
When work measures 18cm/7in from beg, change to 3.25mm needles and work as follows:
Row 1 K2, inc in next st, rib to end.
Row 2 Rib to last 8 sts, inc in next st, p to end.
Row 3 K12, inc in next st, rib to end.
Cont like this, taking 4 more sts into st st on every row and inc in the first/last one before the rib on every row until there are 34 sts in rib for the yoke.
Next row Inc in first and every foll 4th st to 100 sts.
Next row Cast on 18 sts for underfacing, p18, sl1, p to end.
Cont in st st for 18cm/7in, ending with RS facing.

SHAPE ARMHOLES
Cast off 6 sts at beg of next row.
Dec 1 st at same edge of every row 7 times and every alt row 3 times. *(102 sts.)*
Cont until front measures 40cm/15½in from cast-on edge, ending with RS facing.
Row 1 P2, k1, k2tog, p2tog twice, k2tog twice, p2tog twice, k to end.
Row 2 P18, sl1, p to last 22 sts, p2tog twice, k2tog twice, p2tog twice, rib to end.
Row 3 Rib 16, p2tog twice, k2tog twice, p2tog twice, k to end.

Row 4 P18, sl1, p to last 30 sts, k2tog twice, p2tog twice, rib to end.

Row 5 Rib 26, k2tog twice, p2tog twice, k to end.

Row 6 P18, sl1, p17, p2, k2tog, k1, p2tog twice, rib to end.

Row 7 Change to 2.75mm needles, rib to last 36 sts, k36.

Row 8 P18, sl1, p17, rib to end.

Cont in this way until work measures 51cm/20in from beg.

SHAPE SHOULDERS

Cast off 9 sts at armhole edge of next and foll row.

Work 1 row, cast off 10 sts at armhole edge of next and foll row.

Work 5cm/2in in st st on rem 36 sts.

Cast off.

RIGHT FRONT

As left front for 12 rows.

Make buttonholes (see page 137).

Buttonhole row 1 Rib 4, cast off 4 sts, rib to end.

Buttonhole row 2 Rib 68, cast on 4 sts, rib to end.

Cont in rib, making buttonholes as above every 5cm/2in and inc at side edge as on left front every 6th row.

When rib measures 18cm/7in, change to 3.25mm needles and cont as for left front, reversing shapings.

When st st section measures 5cm/2in, make first buttonhole in front facing.

Buttonhole row 1 With RS facing, k10, cast off 4 sts, k7, cast off 4 sts, k to end.

Buttonhole row 2 Purl to where each set of sts were cast off and cast on 4 sts, p to end.

Make two more buttonholes spaced at 5cm/2in intervals.

Cont as for left front, reversing shapings.

BACK

Using 2.75mm needles, cast on 118 sts.

Row 1 *K2, p2, rep from * to end, ending k2.

Row 2 *P2, k2, rep from * to end, ending p2.

Rep these 2 rows until work measures 13cm/5in.

Cont in rib, inc at beg and end of every 6th row until there are 128 sts.

When work measures 18cm/7in, change to 3.25mm needles and st st. Cont until work measures 18cm/7in from top of rib.

SHAPE ARMHOLES

Cast off 4 sts at beg of next 2 rows.

Dec 1 st at each end of every row 6 times. *(108 sts.)*

Cont until st st section measures same as on fronts.

Change to 2.75mm needles and rib until back measures 51cm/20in from beg.

Cast off 9 sts at beg of next 8 rows.

Cast off rem 36 sts.

Join shoulder seams. Sew ends of collar together and sew underfacings in place on WS, stitching collar to back of neck.

SLEEVES

Using 2.75mm needles, cast on 52 sts and work k2, p2 rib for 5cm/2in.

Change to 3.25mm needles and st st.

Work 5 rows, inc on next and every foll 10th row to 70 sts, then every 6th row to 92 sts.

Cont until sleeve measures 48cm/19in.

SHAPE TOP OF SLEEVE

Cast off 4 sts at beg of next 2 rows.

Dec 1 st at each end of every alt row to 42 sts, then every row to 32 sts. Cast off.

Work a second sleeve in the same way.

FINISHING

Block or press carefully, as given on page 137.

Set in sleeves. Join side and sleeve seams.

Work buttonhole stitch around the buttonholes in front facings. Sew on buttons to match buttonholes.

Starlet Sweaters

These are the type of stylish sweaters that were made and worn by women who admired and copied the fashions of the Hollywood stars, so popular during the 1940s and 1950s. The shapes are figure-flattering and feminine, and the patterned Fair Isle, textured and lace stitches of this era – together with the lovely details of collars and buttons on the shoulder or at the back of the neck – make the designs unmistakeably vintage. We have used a selection of luxurious yarns, including cashmere, alpaca and silk, to bring the sweaters up to date for the modern wardrobe. Whether you are at leisure at home, going to work, or entertaining in the evening, these sweaters will see you through, mixing and matching with skirts, trousers and suits. Wearing any one of these designs will give you an affinity with the alluring stars of yesterday, as well as lending you a touch of their star appeal. How could you resist?

This pattern is truly a 1940s treasure. The straight-across neckline was a typical fashion hallmark of the day. The figure-hugging shape and slim sleeves are due to the ribbed stitch, which is set off by panels of bows. This design has all the fashion details that would have been popular in its era, but remains just as elegant today. Knitted in a lovely merino and cashmere mix, this sweater will add to any wardrobe and team with all your skirts and trousers. It will surely become a favourite.

Clara Bow-Panel Sweater

Materials

YARN

7 x 50g balls Rowan Cashsoft 4ply (57% extra fine merino, 33% acrylic microfibre, 10% cashmere, approximately 180m/197 yards), shade 459 Toxic

NEEDLES

1 pair needles size 3mm
1 pair needles size 3.25mm
Stitch holder

SPECIAL ABBREVIATION

bow make bow patt as follows: put point of RH needle over to RS of work and slip it through front loop of next st 9 rows lower down (first row of reverse st st band). Lift this loop up and put it onto LH needle, then k through this loop and next st on LH needle together

MEASUREMENTS

To fit sizes Small [Medium, Large]
Actual chest size 89 [96.5, 106.5]cm/35 [38, 42]in
Length to back neck 53 [58, 61]cm/21 [22¾, 24]in
Underarm sleeve 46 [47, 48]cm/18 [18½, 19]in

TENSION

28 stitches and 36 rows measure 10cm/4in over pattern on 3.25mm needles (or size needed to obtain given tension)

BACK

Using 3mm needles, cast on 119 [129, 145] sts and work in k1, p1 rib as follows:
Row 1 K1, *p1, k1, rep from * to end.
Row 2 P1, *k1, p1, rep from * to end.
Rep these 2 rows for 9cm/3½in, ending with row 2.
Change to 3.25mm needles and commence pattern.
Pattern row 1 (RS) Work 24 [28, 34] sts in k1, p1 rib, k18 for st st band, rib 35 [37, 41], k18 for second st st band, rib 24 [28, 34].
Pattern row 2 Rib 24 [28, 34], p18, rib 35 [37, 41], p18, rib 24 [28, 34]. Rep these 2 rows 4 times more.
Now reverse st st bands as follows:
Pattern row 11 Rib 24 [28, 34], p18, rib 35 [37, 41], p18, rib 24 [28, 34].
Pattern row 12 Rib 24 [28, 34], p18, rib 35 [37, 41], k18, rib 24 [28, 34].
Pattern rows 13–19 Rep patt rows 11 and 12 three times, then rep row 11.
Pattern row 20 (WS) rib 24 [28, 34], k7, *bow*. Rep from * to * 3 times more, k7, rib 35 [37, 41], k7, then rep from * to * 4 times, k7, rib 24 [28, 34].
These 20 rows form the pattern.

Keeping patt as set, inc at each end of every 4th row until there are 147 [155, 171] sts on needle.
Cont straight until back measures 31 [35, 37]cm/ 12 [13¾, 14½]in from beg.

SHAPE ARMHOLES

Keeping cont of patt, shape armholes as follows:

Cast off 13 [15, 19] sts at beg of next 2 rows, then k2tog at beg of next 14 [16, 20] rows. *(107 [109, 113] sts.)*
Cont in patt until armholes measure 18 [19, 20]cm/ 7 [7½, 8]in.
Work 8 rows in k1, p1 rib.

SHAPE SHOULDERS
Cast off 6 sts at beg of next 10 rows. Cast off remainder in rib for neck.

FRONT
Work exactly as given for back until armholes measure 18 [19, 20]cm/7 [7½, 8]in.
Cont in rib as for back.
Cast off 6 sts, rib 24, turn and work back. Leave rem sts on stitch holder.
Cast off 6 sts at beg of next and foll 2 alt rows. Work 1 more row. Cast off.
Return to sts left on stitch holder, cast off 47 [49, 53] sts in rib, patt to end. Work other side to match, reversing shapings.

SLEEVES
Using 3mm needles, cast on 57 [59, 63] sts and work in k1, p1 rib, as given for back.
When work measures 9cm/3½in, change to 3.25mm needles and cont in k1, p1 rib, but inc at each end of every 4th row until there are 111 [117, 129] sts on needle.
Work straight until sleeve measures 46 [47, 48]cm/ 18 [18½, 19]in.

SHAPE TOP OF SLEEVE
Cast off 7 sts at beg of each of next 2 rows, then k2tog at beg of every row until there are 75 [70, 70] sts, then at both ends of every row until 27 sts rem. Cast off.

Work a second sleeve in the same way.

FINISHING
Lay work out flat and press 'bow panels' only, very lightly on WS, as given on page 137. Join shoulder seams and sew sleeves into armholes. Sew up side and sleeve seams.

This lovely vintage pattern from the 1940s has many fashionable features of the period. Fair Isle-type patterns were all the rage, being both very decorative as well as warm. The buttons along the shoulders and the slightly puffed sleeves are also style details from that era. The chart we have made for you is easy to follow and the alpaca yarn in pretty colours sets off the classic pattern to best effect.

Vivien Fair Isle-Style Sweater

Materials

YARN
Artesano 4ply 100% Superfine Alpaca (100% superfine alpaca, approximately 184m/204 yards):
3 [4, 5] x 50g balls, shade SFN10 Cream (A)
1 [1, 2] x 50g balls, shade C743 Fern (B)
1 [2, 2] x 50g balls, shade CA13 Sweet Pea (C)
1 [2, 2] x 50g balls, shade C864 Forget-me-not (D)

NEEDLES
1 pair needles size 3.25mm
1 pair needles size 3.75mm
1 pair needles size 4.5mm

NOTIONS
6 buttons, 1.25cm/½in in diameter

MEASUREMENTS
To fit Small [Medium, Large]
Actual chest size 81 [91, 101]cm
33 [37, 41]in
Length to back neck 50 [52, 54]cm
18½ [20½, 21]in
Underarm sleeve 16 [17, 18]cm
6 [6½, 7]in

TENSION
24 stitches and 28 rows measure 10cm/4in over pattern on 4.5mm needles (or size needed to obtain given tension)

FRONT
Using 3.25mm needles and yarn A, cast on 103 [123, 145] sts.
Row 1 Sl1 k-wise, *p1, k1, rep from * to end.
Row 2 Sl1 k-wise, *k1, p1, rep from * to last 2 sts, k2.
Rep rows 1 and 2 until work measures 5cm/2in, ending with row 1.
Small: Next row (Rib 4, m1) 20 times, rib 3. *(123 sts.)*
Medium: Next row Rib 4, m1, (rib 5) 23 times, rib 4. *(147 sts.)*
Large: Next row Rib 10, m1 (rib 5, m1) 25 times, rib 10. *(171 sts.)*
Change to 3.75mm needles.
Now follow chart on page 72 for pattern (see also page 137) until first band of pink motif has been completed.
Change to size 4.5mm needles and cont until work measures 32cm/12½in from beg.

SHAPE ARMHOLES
Keeping patt as set, cast off 8 sts at beg of next 2 rows.
Keeping patt as set, k2tog at both ends of following alt rows until 87 (107, 127) sts rem.
Cont until armhole measures 19 [21, 23]cm/7½ [8, 9]in from cast-off row.
Change to 3.25mm needles.
Next row Rib 27 (37, 47), cast off 33 sts in rib, rib to end.
Next row Rib back to neck, then make buttonholes on foll row as follows:
Buttonhole row K1, (k2tog, yrn, rib 6 [8, 10]) 3 times, rib to end.
Rib 2 more rows. Cast off in rib.
Work opposite shoulder to match, reversing buttonholes as follows:
Buttonhole row Rib 8, (yf, k2tog, rib 6 [8, 10]) twice, yf, k2tog, k1.

BACK

Work as given for front, omitting buttonholes on shoulders.

SLEEVES

Using 3.25mm needles and yarn A, cast on 79 [99, 119] sts.
Rep rows 1 and 2 of rib given for front 5 times, then
row 1 once.

Small: Next row K1 (inc in next st, rib 3) 19 times, inc in
next st, k1. *(99 sts.)*

Medium: Next row (K4, m1) 24 times, k3. *(123 sts.)*

Large: Next row K6, m1, (k4, m1) 27 times, k5. *(147 sts.)*
Change to 4.5mm needles and cont working from chart
until you end on the patt row that is before armhole
shaping on back and front.

Shape armholes as given for the front. *(63 [83, 103] sts.)*

Cont working from chart but work 2 tog at both ends of
next 5 [7, 9] rows.

Work 2 rows straight, then work 2 tog at both ends of next
3 [5, 7] rows. Cast off.

Work another sleeve in the same way.

FINISHING

Block or press carefully, as given on page 137.

Sew up side and underarm seams.

Place front shoulders to overlap the back by the width
of the rib.

Sew in sleeves, placing seam to seam and centre of cast-off
sts to centre of shoulder ribbing, easing in the fullness at
the top, and matching pattern of front and back.

Sew on buttons to match buttonholes.

KEY

☐ A Cream

▨ B Fern

▨ C Sweet Pea

☐ D Forget-me-not

Read all the knit rows from right to left, and the purl rows
from left to right.

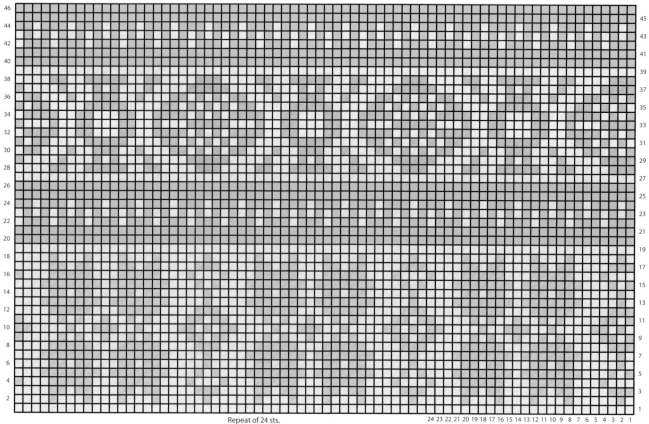

Repeat of 24 sts.

24 23 22 21 20 19 18 17 16 15 14 13 12 11 10 9 8 7 6 5 4 3 2 1

The late 1930s or early 1940s is the era that this sweater hales from; the neat collar, keyhole neckline and slightly puffed sleeves are all hallmarks of that time. We have made the sleeves longer than the original, so that the sweater is more versatile — and because we can afford to be a bit more extravagant with yarn than in those times of austerity. The openwork panels on the front and shoulders give textural interest, which also emphasizes the neckline, all features of the vintage look.

Grace Lacy Puff-Sleeve Sweater

Materials

YARN
7 x 50g balls Sublime Extra Fine Merino Wool 4ply (100% extra fine merino wool, approximately 175m/191 yards), shade 173 Passion

NEEDLES
1 pair needles size 2.75mm
1 pair needles size 3.75mm
1 crochet hook size 2.5mm

NOTIONS
1 button, 1cm/½in in diameter

SPECIAL ABBREVIATION
ssk slip 1, slip 1, as if to knit, insert LH needle into front of these 2 sts from L to R, then knit together

MEASUREMENTS
To fit Small [Medium, Large]
Actual chest size 89 [96, 104]cm
35 [38, 41]in
Length to back neck 55 [58, 61]cm
21 [22¾, 24]in
Underarm sleeve 28cm/11in all sizes

TENSION
28 stitches and 36 rows measure 10cm/4in over stocking stitch on 3.75mm needles (or size needed to obtain given tension)

FRONT
Using 2.75mm needles, cast on 112 [122, 132] sts and work k1, p1 rib for 11cm/4½in.

Change to 3.75mm needles and work as follows:
Row 1 (RS) K37 [42, 47], *p2, k2, k2tog, yf, k3, rep from * 3 times, p2, k37 [42, 47].
Row 2 P37 [42, 47], *k2, p7, rep from * 3 times, k2, p37 [42, 47].
Row 3 K37 [42, 47], *p2, k1, k2tog, yf, k1, yf, ssk, k1, rep from * 3 times, p2, k37 [42, 47].
Row 4 As row 2.
Row 5 K37 [42, 47], *p2, k2tog, yf, k3, yf, ssk, rep from * 3 times, p2, k37 [42, 47].
Row 6 As row 2.
These 6 rows form the pattern.
Rep from row 1, but inc at each end of every 10th row until there are 126 [136, 146] sts. Work without further shaping until you have completed 14th patt from commencement.

SHAPE ARMHOLES
Cast off 6 sts at beg of next 2 rows and dec 1 st at both ends of next 4 rows, 2 sts in from edge. (106 [116, 126] sts.)
Commence yoke and divide sts for front opening as follows:
Row 1 of yoke K2, k2tog, yf, k3, *p2, k2, k2tog, yf, k3, rep from * 4 times, p1, turn.
Slip rem 53 [58, 63] sts onto spare needle and work on first set as follows:
Row 2 of yoke K1, *p7, k2, rep from * until 7 sts rem, p7.
Row 3 of yoke K1, k2tog, yf, k1, yf, ssk, k1, *p2, k1, k2tog, yf, k1, yf, ssk, k1, rep from * 4 times, p1.

Row 4 of yoke As row 2.
Row 5 of yoke K2tog, yf, k3, yf, ssk, *p2, k2tog, yf, k3, yf, ssk, rep from * 4 times, p1.
Row 6 of yoke As row 2.
Rep these 6 rows once more, then work first 5 rows again.

SHAPE NECK
Next row Keeping patt correct, cast off 9 sts, then work as row 2 of yoke to end.
Dec 1 st at neck edge of next 7 rows. (37 [42, 47] sts.)
Keeping patt correct, work 34 rows.

SHAPE SHOULDER
Cast off 12 [13, 14] sts at beg of next and foll alt row and 13 [14, 15] sts at beg of foll row.
Join yarn to inner edge of sts on spare needle, and work other side to match, reversing shaping.

BACK
Using 2.75mm needles, cast on 112 [122, 132] sts and work k1, p1 rib for 11cm/4½in.
Change to 3.75mm needles and work in st st, but inc at each end of every 10th row until there are 126 [136, 146] sts.

Work straight until work measures same as front to armhole shaping.

SHAPE ARMHOLES
Cast off 6 sts at beg of next 2 rows and dec 1 st at each end of next 4 rows. (106 [116, 126] sts.)
Work without further dec until armhole measures 18cm/7in, then shape shoulders by casting off 12 [13, 14] sts at beg of next and foll alt row and 13 [14, 15] sts at beg of foll row.
Leave rem sts for back of neck on a spare needle.

SLEEVES
Using 2.75mm needles, cast on 76 [82, 88] sts and work in k1, p1 rib for 10 rows.
Change to 3.75mm needles and cont in st st, inc at each end of every 10th row until there are 82 [88, 94] sts on needle.
Work straight until sleeve measures 28cm/11in.

SHAPE TOP OF SLEEVE
Cast off 6 sts at beg of next 2 rows. Work 23 rows then dec 1 st at each end of next row. (68 [74, 80] sts.)
Work straight until cap measures 14 [17, 19]cm/ 5½ [6½, 7½]in.
Dec 1 st at each end of every alt row 6 [7, 10] times. (56 [60, 60] sts.)
To get the gathered effect for the top of the sleeve cap, you will be reducing the number of sts by half over the next row, then half again on the foll row, as follows:
K2tog across next row. P2tog across foll row.
Cast off rem 14 [15, 15] sts loosely.
Work a second sleeve in the same way.

COLLAR
Join shoulder seams of sweater. Then, using 2.75mm needles, pick up and k 120 [128, 136] sts around neck edge, including sts left on spare needle at back of neck.
Row 1 P1, *k1, p1, rep from * to end.
Row 2 K1, *p1, k1, rep from * to end.
Rep these 2 rows until you have worked 16 rows.
Change to 3.75mm needles and work 18 rows.
Cast off in rib.

FINISHING
Block or press carefully, as given on page 137. Sew sleeves into armholes, gathering in tops to fit. Join side and sleeve seams. Using crochet hook, make a 3 or 4ch buttonhole loop to take 1cm/½in button at top of front opening on RH side, and sew button to LH side.

This lovely vintage pattern, knitted in luxurious pure silk, was originally introduced 'with a new neckline'; the collar is set wide apart and finished with a ribbed neck that is echoed on the shoulders and yoke. The buttons at the back of the neck are a vintage detail that adds charm to this beautiful 1940s sweater. Why leave this gorgeous pattern lingering in the archives of a bygone age when it is so attractive and wearable today? You will be sure to get admiring glances.

Marlene Lacy Sweater with Collar

Materials

YARN
8 [9, 10] x 50g balls Louisa Harding Mulberry (100% silk, approximately 124m/136 yards), shade 12 Olive Green

NEEDLES
1 pair needles size 2.75mm
1 pair needles size 3.25mm
1 crochet hook size 2.5mm
Stitch holder

NOTIONS
4 buttons, 1cm/½in in diameter

MEASUREMENTS
To fit Small [Medium, Large]
Actual chest size (slightly stretched) 82 [88, 94]cm
32 [34½, 37]in
Length to back neck 50 [54, 58]cm
20 [21, 23]in
Underarm sleeve 50cm/20in all sizes

TENSION
30 stitches and 34 rows measure 10cm/4in over pattern on 3.25mm needles (or size needed to obtain given tension)

BACK
****Using 2.75mm needles, cast on 111 [121, 131] sts.
Work in k1, p1 rib for 9cm/3½in.
Next row
Small *K8, m1, (k5, m1) to last 8 sts, k8. *(131 sts.)*
Medium K4, m1, (k6, m1) to last 3 sts, k3. *(141 sts.)*
Large K9, m1, (k6, m1) to last 8 sts, k8. *(151 sts.)*
Next row Purl.
Change to 3.25mm needles and commence pattern.
Row 1 K1, *yf, k3, k3tog, k3, yf, k1, rep from * to end of row.
Row 2 Purl.
Row 3 As Row 1.
Row 4 Knit.
These 4 rows form the pattern.
Rep patt rows until work measures approximately 32 [34, 36]cm/12½ [13, 14]in, ending with row 4 of patt.

SHAPE ARMHOLES
Row 1 Cast off 7 sts, k3, *yf, k3, k3tog, k3, yf, k1, rep from * to end of row.
Row 2 Cast off 7 sts, p to end of row.
Row 3 K2tog, k2, *yf, k3, k3tog, k3, yf, k1, rep from * to last 3 sts, k1, k2tog.
Row 4 K2tog, k to last 2 sts, k2tog.
Row 5 K2tog, *yf, k3, k3tog, k3, yf, k1, rep from * to end of row, but finish last rep with k2tog instead of k1. *(91 [101, 111] sts.)*
Cont in patt until work measures approx 6.5 [7, 7]cm/ 2½ [3, 3]in from beg of armhole shaping, ending with row 4 of patt.****

YOKE

Row 1 (RS) K1, p1 to last st, k1.

Row 2 P1, k1 to last st, p1.

Next row K1, p1 over 44 [49, 54] sts, k2tog, turn, slipping the rem 45 [50, 55] sts onto a stitch holder.
**Cont on sts on needle in k1, p1 rib until armhole measures 15 [17, 19]cm/6 [6½, 7]in from beg of armhole shaping.

SHAPE SHOULDER

Cast off 10 [11, 10] sts at beg of each of the next 3 [3, 4] alt rows at armhole end. Cast off rem sts. **
Rejoin yarn to neck end of 45 [50, 55] sts on stitch holder, and work as from ** to ** of first side.

FRONT

Work as for back from **** to ****.

YOKE

Work in k1, p1 rib across all sts for 6 rows.

Next row Rib 30 [33, 40] sts, cast off next 31 [35, 31] sts, then rib to end of row.

Working only over the last set of sts, rib until armhole measures same as back to shoulder.

SHAPE SHOULDER

Cast off 10 [11, 10] sts at beg of each of next 3 [3, 4] alt rows at armhole end.

Rejoin yarn to inner edge of second group of sts and work to match first side, reversing shaping.

SLEEVES

Using 2.75mm needles, cast on 50 [60, 60] sts, and work in k1, p1 rib for 7.5cm/3in, inc 1 st at end of last row.
(51 [61, 61] sts.)

Change to 3.25mm needles and commence patt rows.
Work 8 complete patts.

Keeping cont of patt where possible and working any extra sts in st st, inc at each end of next row and every 4th patt row after until there are 85 [90, 95] sts.

Cont without shaping until sleeve measures 50cm/20in.

SHAPE TOP OF SLEEVE

Dec 1 st at both ends of every row for 32 [34, 36] rows.
(21 [22, 23] sts.)

Cast off.

Work another sleeve in the same way.

COLLAR

Work 2 alike, as follows:

Using 2.75mm needles, cast on 43 [47, 51] sts, and work in k1, p1 rib for 2 rows.

Then, keeping cont of ribbing, inc 1 st at both ends of the next row and every alt row until there are 65 [69, 73] sts. Cast off loosely.

FINISHING

Block or press carefully, as given on page 137.

Join shoulder seams and sew sleeves into armholes.

Join side and sleeve seams.

Placing one end of collar at back neck opening, sew cast-on edges of collar in position, so that collar ends just above front neck ribbing.

Using crochet hook, work 1 row of dc along back opening, making 4 buttonholes of 3ch evenly spaced in LH side (see page 139).

Sew on buttons to match buttonholes.

The sensual touch of cashmere makes this sleeveless sweater irresistible to wear. It has attractive panels of openwork over the shoulders and cap sleeves and around the neck; the high, patterned neckline is made to fit close by the button opening at the back of the neck. Originally a pattern from the early 1950s, it would have been worn as a sleeveless 'shell' top, but it also works well over a blouse or long-sleeved top, as shown here. Either way, it is the perfect versatile addition to a modern wardrobe.

Audrey Leaf-Pattern Sweater

Materials

YARN
5 x 50g balls Bergere de France Origin Cachemire (90% cashmere/10% wool, approximately 150m/164 yards), shade 242.65 Luxe

NEEDLES
1 pair needles size 2.25mm
1 pair needles size 3mm
1 pair needles size 3.25mm
1 pair needles size 3.75mm
Stitch holders

NOTIONS
4 buttons, 1cm/½in in diameter

SPECIAL ABBREVIATION
ssk slip 1, slip 1, as if to knit, insert LH needle into front of these 2 sts from L to R, then knit together
sk2p slip 1, knit 2 together, pass slipped stitch over

MEASUREMENTS
To fit Small [Medium, Large]
Actual chest size 86 [91, 96]cm/34 [36, 38]in
Length to back neck 58 [61, 63]cm/23 [24, 25]in

TENSION
24 stitches and 36 rows measure 10cm/4in over stocking stitch on size 3.75mm needles (or size needed to obtain given tension)

Note: After row 1 is worked, the number of sts is reduced by 2 in each panel, so always count the sts on a row 8.

BACK
Using 3mm needles, cast on 100 [108, 116] sts.
Work in k1, p1 rib for 10cm/4in.
Change to 3.75mm needles and commence pattern.
Row 1 K2, *p2, k1, yf, k1, ssk, p1, k2tog, k1, p1, k1, ssk, p1, k2tog, k1, yf, k1.* Rep from * to * once. P2, k16 [24, 32], rep from * to * twice, p2, k2.
Row 2 P2, *k2, p4, (k1, p2) twice, k1, p4.* Rep from * to * once. K2, p16 [24, 32], rep from * to * twice, k2, p2.
Row 3 K2, *p2, k1, yf, k1, yf, ssk, p1, k2tog, p1, ssk, p1, k2tog, (yf, k1) twice.* Rep from * to * once. P2, k16 [24, 32], rep from * to * twice, p2, k2.
Row 4 P2, *k2, p5, (k1, p1) twice, k1, p5.* Rep from * to * once. K2, p16 [24, 32], rep from * to * twice, k2, p2.
Row 5 K2, *p2, k1, yf, k3, yf, sk2p, p1, sk2p, yf, k3, yf, k1.* Rep from * to * once. P2, k16 [24, 32], rep from * to * twice, p2, k2.
Row 6 P2, *k2, p7, k1, p7.* Rep from * to * once. K2, p16 [24, 32], rep from * to * twice, k2, p2.
Row 7 K2, *p2, k1, yf, k5, yf, sk2p, yf, k5, yf, k1.* Rep from * to * once. P2, k16 [24, 32], rep from * to * twice, p2, k2.
Row 8 P2, *k2, p17.* Rep from * to * once. K2, p16 [24, 32], rep from * to * twice, k2, p2.
These 8 rows form the pattern.
Cont in patt, inc 1 st at beg and end of each row and in 2nd and 2nd last st of centre st st panel on every row 8 to 124 [132, 140] sts. Then inc in centre panel only to 128 [136, 144] sts.
Cont until work measures 34cm/13½in, ending after a row 8.

SHAPE ARMHOLES

Next row Cast off 8 sts, work patt as row 1 from * to * twice, p2, work centre st st panel, still inc as before, then cont in patt to end.

Next row Cast off 8 sts, work in patt as row 2.

Cont to inc in centre panel as before 3 times more. *(118 [126, 134] sts.)*

Cont until work measures 42cm/16½in from beg.

DIVIDE FOR BACK OPENING

Next row Work patt for 57 [61, 65] sts, (p1, k1) twice, turn, leaving rem 57 [61, 65] sts on stitch holder.

Next row (P1, k1) twice, work patt to end.

Keeping patt as set, work the 4 centre back sts in rib and cont the incs as before.

When 10 rows have been worked, make buttonhole as follows:

Work patt to last 4 sts, p1, yf, k2tog, k1.

Work 8 more rows in patt and then rep the buttonhole in the 9th row.

Repeat these 9 rows once more.

Cont until the last inc has been made, and there are 64 [68, 72] sts on the inc row.

Cont to approximately 19cm/7½in from beg of armhole shaping, ending after a row 8.

SHAPE SHOULDER

Cast off 20 [22, 24] sts at beg of next row and 19 [21, 23] sts at beg of foll alt row. Rejoin yarn to rem sts.

Cast on 4 sts, work (k1, p1) twice, then complete in patt to match other side, reversing shaping and omitting the buttonholes.

FRONT

Work as for back until armholes measure 16cm/6¼in and there are 34 [42, 50] sts in centre panel.

SHAPE NECK

Work patt over 40 sts, k11 [15, 19], knit next 12 and put them on stitch holder, k11 [15, 19], patt to end.

Cont in patt, dec 1 st at neck edge in the next 11 rows, then foll alt row.

Cont until armhole measures same as for back, ending at armhole edge.

SHAPE SHOULDER

As for back.

NECKBAND

Join shoulder seams.

Using 3mm needles and with RS facing, rib 4, then k 22 [25, 28] sts from left back holder, pick up and k 21 [22, 23] sts

down left front neck edge, k12 from front neck holder, k 21 [22, 23] sts up right front neck edge, k 22 [25, 28] sts from right back neck holder, rib 4. Change to 3.25mm needles.

Next row Rib 4, p49, p2tog, p to last 4, rib 4.

Next row Rib 4, then work row 1 of patt from * to *, to last 6 sts, p2, rib 4.

Cont in patt as set with 4 sts at each end in rib for 10 rows, making 1 more buttonhole, as given before, on RH side of back opening.

Change to 2.25mm needles and work 4 rows in k1, p1 rib, working p2tog where there are 2 purl sts between leaves.

Make another buttonhole on 2nd row. Cast off loosely in rib.

SLEEVE BANDS

Using 3mm needles and with RS facing, knit up 99 [103, 107] sts around armholes.

Work in k1, p1 rib for 2.5cm/1in. Cast off loosely in rib.

FINISHING

Block or press carefully, as given on page 137.

Sew side edges of sleeve bands to cast-off edges of underarms. Join side seams. Slipstitch LH facing of back at lower edge. Sew on buttons to match buttonholes.

The delicate feather stitch used here — so easy to knit — enhances a fine alpaca sweater taken straight from the 1950s archive; the only thing we have changed for you is to make a new scooped neckline. This pattern would also work well in pastel colours, or in a similar weight cotton. Suitable for any occasion, this little sweater can go from smart to casual, depending on how you wear it. The shape is really flattering, so it is sure to be a much-loved and versatile piece.

Natalie Feather-Stitch Sweater

Materials

YARN
6 [7, 9] x 50g balls Artesano 4ply 100% Superfine Alpaca (100% superfine alpaca, approximately 184m/204 yards), shade SFN24 Demerera

NEEDLES
1 pair needles size 3.25mm
1 pair needles size 3.75mm
1 circular needle size 3.25mm
Stitch holders

MEASUREMENTS
To fit Small [Medium, Large]
Actual chest size 81 [89, 96.5]cm
32 [35, 38]in
Length to back neck 55 [58, 61]cm
21½ [22¾, 24]in
Underarm sleeve 43cm/17in all sizes

TENSION
24 stitches and 26 rows measure 10cm/4in over pattern on 3.75mm needles (or size needed to obtain given tension)

BACK
Using 3.25mm needles, cast on 92 [106, 118] sts loosely.
Work in k2, p2 rib for 7.5cm/3in, inc 2 [1, 2] sts on last row. *(94 [107, 120] sts.)*
Change to 3.75mm needles and pattern.
Row 1 Knit.
Row 2 Purl.
Row 3 K1, p1, *k2tog twice, (m1, k1) 4 times, k2tog twice, p1, rep from * to last st, k1.
Row 4 Purl.
These 4 rows form the pattern.
Rep these 4 rows until work measures 38 [40, 42]cm/ 15 [16, 16½]in.

SHAPE ARMHOLES
Row 1 Cast off 5 sts at beg of next 2 rows, keeping patt correct.
Then dec 1 st at beg and end of every alt row to 80 [86, 92] sts.
Cont without shaping until armhole measures 20 [21, 22]cm/8 [8¼, 8½]in.

SHAPE SHOULDER
Row 1 Cast off 11 [12, 13] sts at beg of next 4 rows.
Leave these 36 [38, 40] sts on stitch holder.

FRONT
Work as for back until armhole measures 6cm/2½in with 80 [86, 92] sts rem.

SHAPE NECK

Work 31 [33, 35] sts.

Slip next 18 [20, 22] sts onto a stitch holder.

Work rem 31 [33, 35] sts.

Dec 1 st at neck edge of every row 9 times, until 22 [24, 26] sts rem.

Keeping patt correct, work until armhole measures 20 [21, 22]cm/8 [8¼, 8½]in.

SHAPE SHOULDER

Cast off 11 [12, 13] sts at beg of next and foll alt row.

Return to first set of sts and work other side to match.

SLEEVE

Using 3.25mm needles, cast on 42 [42, 55] sts.

Work in k1, p1 rib for 5cm/2in.

Change to 3.75mm needles and patt as for back.

Keeping patt correct, but working in st st when there are too few sts to take into patt, inc 1 st at each end of 5th row, then every 6th row. *(74 [78, 87] sts.)*

Cont until sleeve measures 43cm/17in.

SHAPE TOP OF SLEEVE

Cast off 5 sts at beg of next 2 rows.

Dec 1 st at each end of every row 4 times.

Dec 1 st at each end of every alt row 13 times.

Dec 1 st at each end of every row 4 [4, 6] times.

Cast off rem 22 [26, 31] sts loosely.

Work a second sleeve in the same way.

FINISHING

Block or press carefully, as given on page 137.

Sew up shoulder seams.

With RS facing and using the circular 3.25mm needle, pick up and k 36 [38, 40] sts from back neck stitch holder, 40 [44, 48] sts from left front neck edge, 18 [20, 22] sts from front neck stitch holder and 40 [44, 48] sts from right front neck edge. *(134 [146, 158] sts.)*

Work 2.5cm/1in (8 rows) in k1, p1 rib.

Cast off loosely.

Twinsets & Two-Pieces

The twinset must be one of the only fashion statements that has lasted more than fifty years. Originally seen in the 1940s, it has been sometimes glamorous, worn by stars such as Grace Kelly and Audrey Hepburn, and other times smart, practical and preppy, sported by girl-next-door secretaries or teachers; it has managed to span the worlds of Hollywood and the workplace. The designs we have chosen are decorated with lace stitches or cables, in real 1940s style. Wearing a short-sleeved sweater together with a cardigan gives extra warmth, but still looks good when the top layer is removed, which is one of the reasons the versatile twinset was, and still remains, so popular. The beautiful cotton lace blouse and skirt (see page 108) is pure 1930s and another form of two-piece. Looser and less tailored than the 1940s styles to come, it is graceful and elegant with period appeal, but sophisticated enough to outlast many more modern, but short-lived, styles.

The square neck and three little cables on this short-sleeved sweater complement its matching cardigan and make a stunning twinset. The low V and neat waist—classic 1940s styling—make the cardigan as wearable today as when it was designed. The lovely fine merino wool 4ply comes in such a beautiful colour range that you will be spoiled for choice.

Barbara Fine Cable Twinset

Materials

YARN

16 x 50g balls Sublime Extra Fine Merino Wool 4ply (100% merino wool, approx 175m/191 yards), shade 017 Redcurrant

NEEDLES

1 pair needles size 2.75mm; 1 pair needles size 3.25mm; 1 cable needle; safety pins

NOTIONS

3 buttons, 1cm/½in in diameter

SPECIAL ABBREVIATIONS

C3f slip 2 knit sts onto cable needle in front of work, p1, then k2 sts off cable needle

C3b slip 1 purl st onto cable needle at back of work, k2, then p1 off cable needle

C4 slip 2 knit sts onto cable needle at back of work, k2, then k2 sts off cable needle

ssk slip 1, slip 1, as if to knit, insert LH needle into front of these 2 sts from L to R, then knit together

MEASUREMENTS

To fit Small [Medium, Large]

Sweater Actual chest size 81 [91, 101]cm/32 [36, 40]in

Length to back neck 47 [49, 51]cm/18½ [19, 20]in

Underarm sleeve 11cm/4½in all sizes

Cardigan Actual chest size 81 [91, 101]cm/32 [36, 40]in

Length to back neck 48 [50, 52]cm/19 [19½, 20½]in

Underarm sleeve 44cm/17in all sizes

TENSION

32 stitches and 38 rows measure 10cm/4in over pattern on 3.25mm needles (or size needed to obtain given tension)

Sweater

FRONT

Using 2.75mm needles, cast on 96 [112, 128] sts.

Row 1 P1, *k2, p2. Rep from * ending k2, p1.

Row 2 K1, *p2, k2. Rep from * ending p2, k1.

Rep these 2 rows for 9cm/3½in, ending with row 2.

Small: Next row K2, m1, (k4, m1) 23 times, k2. *(120 sts.)*

Medium: Next row K10, m1, (k4, m1) 23 times, k10. *(136 sts.)*

Large: Next row K7, m1, (k5, m1) 23 times, k6. *(152 sts.)*

Change to 3.25mm needles and work in st st, starting with a k row, until work measures 15cm/6in.

With RS facing commence patt:

Row 1 K55 [63, 71], (p2, k2) twice, p2, k55 [63, 71].

Row 2 P55 [63, 71], (k2, p2) twice, k2, p55 [63, 71].

Rep rows 1 and 2 twice more.

Row 7 K55 [63, 71], p2, C3f, C3b, p2, k55 [63, 71].

Row 8 P55 [63, 71], k3, p4, k3, p55 [63, 71].

Row 9 K55 [63, 71], p3, C4, p3, k55 [63, 71].

Row 10 As row 8.

Row 11 K55 [63, 71], p2, C3b, C3f, p2, k55 [63, 71].

Row 12 As row 2.

Rep rows 1 and 2 four times more.

Row 21 As row 7.

Row 22 As row 8.

Row 23 As row 9.

Row 24 As row 8.

Row 25 As row 11.

Row 26 As row 2.

Rep rows 1 and 2 twice.

These 30 rows form the pattern.

Rep from row 1, but bring in side cables as follows:

Next row K35 [43, 51], *(p2, k2) twice, p2, k10; rep from * twice more, k to end.

Cont in patt to 30 [32, 34]cm/12 [12½, 13]in.

SHAPE ARMHOLES

Cast off 9 sts at beg of next 2 rows.

Next row K1, ssk, patt to last 3 sts, k2tog, k1.

Next row P1, p2tog, patt to last 3 sts, p2togtbl, p1.

Rep these 2 rows once more. *(97 [113, 129] sts.)*

Cont in patt until work measures 10cm/4in from beg of armhole shaping.

Next row K22 [30, 38], (p2, k2) 12 times, p2, k22 [30, 38].

Next row P22 [30, 38], (k2, p2) 12 times, k2, p22 [30, 38].

Rep these 2 rows 5 times more.

Next row K22 [30, 38], p2, k2, p2, cast off 38 sts ribwise, p2, k2, p2, k22 [30, 38].

Cont on last 28 [36, 44] sts until work measures 15 [16, 17]cm/6 [6, 7]in from beg of armhole shaping, ending with RS facing.

Cont in p2, k2 rib until work measures 17 [18, 19]cm/ 7 [7, 7½]in from beg of armhole shaping.

SHAPE SHOULDERS

With WS facing, cast off 9 [12, 14] sts at beg of next and foll alt row.

Cast off 10 [12, 16] sts on foll alt row.

Rejoin yarn to rem sts and work other side to match, reversing shaping.

BACK

Work as for front until inc row has been worked.

Change to 3.25mm needles and work in st st until work measures same as front to armholes.

SHAPE ARMHOLES

Work as for front.

When work measures 15 [16, 17]cm/6 [6, 7]in, change to p2, k2 rib and cont until work measures same as front to shoulders.

SHAPE SHOULDERS

Cast off 9 [12, 14] sts at beg of next 4 rows and 10 [12, 16] sts at beg of next 2 rows. Cast off rem sts loosely in rib.

SLEEVES

Using 2.75mm needles, cast on 94 [110, 126] sts.

Row 1 *K2, p2. Rep from * ending k2.

Row 2 *P2, k2. Rep from * ending p2.

Rep these 2 rows for 2.5cm/1in, finishing after a row 2.

Change to 3.25mm needles and st st. Cont until sleeve measures 11cm/4in.

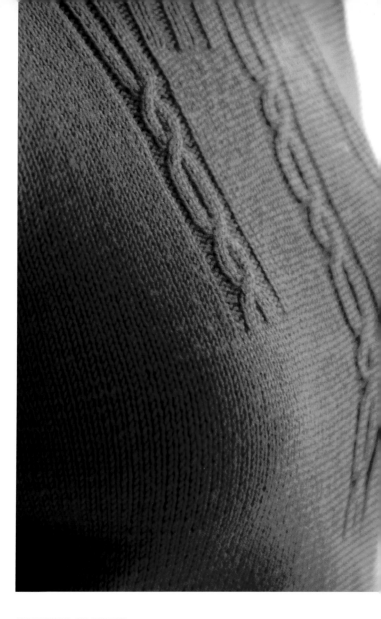

SHAPE TOP OF SLEEVE

Next row K1, ssk, k to last 3 sts, k2tog, k1.

Next row P1, p2tog, p to last 3 sts, p2togtbl, p1.

Rep these 2 rows 4 times more, then dec on alt rows only until sleeve measures 15 [16, 17]cm/6 [6, 7]in from beg of shaping. Cast off rem sts.

Work a second sleeve in the same way.

FINISHING

Block or press carefully, as given on page 137.

Join shoulder seams. Sew side and sleeve seams.

Then arrange sleeves into armholes, with sleeve seams to side seams and any extra fullness gathered at either side of shoulder seams. Press all seams.

Cardigan

BACK

Using 2.75mm needles, cast on 120 [136, 152] sts.
Work rib as for sweater front for 7.5cm/3in, finishing
with a row 2.
Change to 3.25mm needles and work in st st (next row k)
until work measures 31 [33, 35]cm/12 [13, 13½]in.

SHAPE ARMHOLES

Cast off 4 sts at beg of next 2 rows, then dec as for sweater
at each end of foll 9 rows. *(94 [110, 126] sts.)*
Cont on these sts until work measures 48 [50, 52]cm/
19 [19½, 20½]in, finishing on a WS row.

SHAPE SHOULDERS

Cast off 8 [9, 11] sts at beg of next 8 rows. Cast off rem sts.

RIGHT FRONT

Using 2.75mm needles, cast on 68 [76, 84] sts.
Row 1 (K1, p1) 6 times, (k2, p2) to end.
Row 2 (K2, p2) to last 12 sts, (k1, p1) 6 times.
Rep these 2 rows once more.
Make buttonhole (see page 137).
Buttonhole row 1 (K1, p1) 4 times, cast off 3 sts, then rib
to end as set.
Buttonhole row 2 Work back in rib, casting on 3 sts to
replace those cast off.
Cont to rep buttonhole rows 1 and 2, making 2 further
buttonholes 6cm/2in apart.
When rib measures same as on the back, work as follows:
Next row (K1, p1) 6 times.
Place these 12 sts onto a safety pin for band.
Change to 3.25mm needles and place cable, as for sweater,
at front edge as follows:
Row 1 (K2, p2) 3 times (these 12 sts are for cable), k to end.
Cont working cable pattern as for sweater, but inc 1 st at
side edge on every 8th row.
Cont until work measures 30 [32, 34]cm/12 [12½, 13]in.

SHAPE ARMHOLE

With WS facing, cast off 7 sts at beg of next and each alt
row 3 times altogether. *(47 [55, 63] sts.)*
Then dec 1 st at same edge each row as on sweater until
32 [40, 48] sts rem.
Cont on these sts until work measures 48 [50, 52]cm/
19 [19½, 20½]in.

SHAPE SHOULDER

Beg at armhole edge:
Cast off 8 [10, 12] sts at beg of next and each alt row 4 times.

BUTTONHOLE BAND

Rejoin yarn to 12 sts on safety pin at inside edge and, using
2.75mm needles, cont on these sts in k1, p1 rib.
Cont until band, when slightly stretched, reaches halfway
across back neck, then leave on stitch holder to graft or cast
off together with button band.

LEFT FRONT

Using 2.75mm needles, cast on 68 [76, 84] sts.
Row 1 (P2, k2) to within 12 sts, (p1, k1) 6 times.
Row 2 (P1, k1) 6 times, (p2, k2) to end.
Cont as for right front, reversing shapings and
omitting buttonholes.

BUTTON BAND

Work as for buttonhole band.

SLEEVES

Using 2.75mm needles, cast on 60 [68, 76] sts.
Work in k2, p2 rib for 7.5cm/3in.
Change to 3.25mm needles and work in st st, inc 1 st at
each end of every 8th row until sleeve measures 44cm/17in.

SHAPE TOP OF SLEEVE

Next row K1, ssk, k to last 3 sts, k2tog, k1.
Next row P1, p2tog, p to last 3 sts, p2togtbl, p1.
Rep these 2 rows 4 times more, then dec on RS only
until sleeve measures 14 [15, 16]cm/5½ [6, 6]in from
beg of shaping, then dec at each end of next 10 rows.
Cast off rem sts.

FINISHING

Block or press carefully, as given on page 137.
Join shoulder seams. Neatly sew bands up fronts and
join centre back seam. Sew side and sleeve seams.
Then arrange sleeves into armholes, with sleeve seams
2.5cm/1in to front of side seams and any extra sleeve
fullness gathered to either side of shoulder seams.
Sew on buttons to match buttonholes and press all seams.

This elegant pattern from the end of the 1940s is timeless. Knitted in a lace-weight merino wool and silk yarn, which makes up into a fine, delicate fabric, the cardigan is designed to show off the lacy panel on the sweater and repeats the pattern in bands along its front opening.

Celia Lacy Fine-Knit Twinset

Materials

YARN
2 [3, 3] x 100g hanks Fyberspates Scrumptious Lace (55% merino wool, 45% silk, approximately 1000m/1093 yards), shade Water

NEEDLES
1 pair needles size 2.75mm
1 pair needles size 3.25mm
1 crochet hook size 2.5mm

NOTIONS
5 buttons, 1.5cm/⅝in in diameter
3 buttons, 1cm/½in in diameter

SPECIAL ABBREVIATION
ssk slip 1, slip 1, as if to knit, insert LH needle into front of these 2 sts from L to R, then knit together

MEASUREMENTS
To fit Small [Medium, Large]
Actual chest size 82 [92, 102]cm
32 [36, 40]in
Cardigan
Length to back neck 56 [59, 62]cm
22 [23, 24]in
Underarm sleeve 49cm/19in all sizes
Sweater
Length to back neck 50 [53, 56]cm
20 [21, 22]in
Underarm sleeve 18cm/7in all sizes

TENSION
32 stitches and 38 rows measure 10cm/4in over pattern on 3.25mm needles (or size needed to obtain given tension)

Cardigan

RIGHT FRONT

Using 2.75mm needles and yarn double, cast on
64 [72, 80] sts. Change to single yarn.
Row 1 Sl1 k-wise, k6, *k1, p1, rep from * to last st, k1.
Row 2 Sl1 k-wise, *k1, p1, rep from * to last 7 sts, k7.
Rep rows 1 and 2 once.
Row 5 Make buttonhole (see page 137):
Sl1 k-wise, k2, cast off 2 sts, k2, rib to end.
Row 6 Work as row 2, casting on 2 sts above those cast off.
Rep rows 1 and 2 fourteen times, then rows 5 and 6 once.
Change to 3.25mm needles and commence patt as follows:
Row 1 Sl1 k-wise, k6, *k1, p5, k7, p5*, k to end.
Row 2 and every alt row Sl1 k-wise, p to last 7 sts, k7.
Row 3 Sl1 k-wise, k6, *k1, p4, k2tog, k2, yf, k1, yf, k2, ssk,
p4*, k to last st, inc in last st.
Row 5 Sl1 k-wise, k6, *k1, p3, k2tog, k2, yf, k3, yf, k2, ssk,
p3*, k to end.
Row 7 Sl1 k-wise, k6, *k1, p2, k2tog, k2, yf, k5, yf, k2, ssk,
p2*, k to end.
Row 9 Sl1 k-wise, k6, *k1, p1, k2tog, k2, yf, k7, yf, k2, ssk,
p1*, k to end.
Row 10 As row 2.
These 10 rows form the pattern.
Cont in this patt, making further buttonholes on foll 19th
and 20th rows, then on 29th and 30th rows, still inc on
every 10th row.
When there are 69 [77, 85] sts and 5th and last buttonhole
has been made, cont straight until work measures 33 [36,
39]cm/13 [14, 15]in from beg, ending at side edge.

SHAPE ARMHOLE

Cast off 7 sts at beg of next row, then k tog 26th and 27th sts
on next and every foll 4th row, AT THE SAME TIME k2tog
at armhole edge on every row until 45 [53, 61] sts rem.
Keeping armhole edge straight, dec at front only every
4th row until 34 [42, 50] sts rem.
Cont if necessary on these sts until work measures 53 [56,
59]cm/21 [22, 23]in from beg, ending at side edge.
Cast off 9 [11, 10] sts at this edge 3 [3, 4] times.
K straight on rem 7 [9, 10] sts for 5cm/2in. Cast off.

LEFT FRONT

Using 2.75mm needles and yarn double, cast on
64 [72, 80] sts. Change to single yarn.
Row 1 Sl1 k-wise, *p1, k1, rep from * to last 7 sts, k7.
Row 2 Sl1 k-wise, k6, *p1, k1, rep from * to last st, k1.
Rep these 2 rows 17 times.
Change to 3.25mm needles and commence patt:

Row 1 and every alt row Sl1 k-wise, k to last 26 sts,
rep from * to * on corresponding patt row of right
front once, k8.
Row 2 and every alt row Sl1 k-wise, k6, p to last st, k1.
Cont in this way, omitting the buttonholes, inc 1 st at
beg of next and every foll 10th row until there are 69
[77, 85] sts.
Finish to match right side, reversing shapings and working
ssk at front edge.

BACK

Using 2.75mm needles and yarn double, cast on
125 [141, 157] sts. Change to single yarn.
Row 1 Sl1 k-wise, *p1, k1, rep from * to end.
Row 2 Sl1 k-wise, *k1, p1, rep from * to last 2 sts, k2.
Rep these 2 rows 17 times.
Change to 3.25mm needles and st st, inc 1 st at both ends of
3rd and every foll 10th row until there are 133 [149, 165] sts.
Cont straight until work measures same as front to underarm.
Cast off 7 sts at beg of each of next 2 rows, then k2tog at
both ends of every row until 93 [109, 125] sts rem.
Cont straight until armholes are same depth as front armholes.
Cast off 9 [11, 10] sts at beg of each of next 6 [6, 8] rows.
Cast off loosely.

SLEEVES

Using 2.75mm needles and yarn double, cast on
53 [63, 73] sts. Change to single yarn.
Work 7.5cm/3in in rib as for back.
Change to 3.25mm needles and st st, inc 1 st at both
ends of 9th and then every foll 4th row until there are
105 [115, 125] sts.
Cont straight until work measures 49cm/19in.

SHAPE TOP OF SLEEVE

Cast off 6 sts at beg of each of next 2 rows, then k2tog
at both ends of every 2nd row until 47 [57, 67] sts rem.
Cast off.

Work a second sleeve in the same way.

FINISHING

Block or press carefully, as given on page 137.
Join the side, shoulder and sleeve seams.
Sew in sleeves, placing seam to seam.
Join front borders and sew to back of neck.
Sew on buttons to match buttonholes. Press seams.

Sweater

FRONT

Using 2.75mm needles and yarn double, cast on
123 [139, 155] sts. Change to single yarn.
Work 7.5cm/3in in rib, as for cardigan back welt.
Change to 3.25mm needles and st st, inc 1 st at both ends of
next and every foll 6th row until there are 131 [147, 163] sts.
Cont straight until work measures 32 [35, 38]cm/12½ [14,
15]in from beg.
Cast off 10 sts at beg of each of next 2 rows, then k2tog at both
ends of every row until 93 [109, 125] sts rem. Purl one row.
Change to patt as follows:
Row 1 Sl1 k-wise, rep from * to * on corresponding patt
row of right front of the cardigan, to last 2 sts, k2.
Row 2 and every alt row Sl1 k-wise, p to last st, k1.
Rep these 2 rows until 4 complete patts have been worked.
Change to st st until work measures 48cm/19in from beg,
ending with a p row.
Next row Sl1 k-wise, k38 [46, 54], cast off 15 sts, k to end.
Cont on last 39 [47, 55] sts knitting 2 tog at neck edge on
every row until 32 [40, 48] sts rem.
Cont until work measures 50 [53, 56]cm/19½ [21, 22]in
from beg, ending at armhole edge.
Cast off 8 [10, 12] sts at this edge 4 times.
Join yarn and work other side to match, reversing shapings.

BACK

Work as for front until yoke patt has been worked 3 times.
Divide for back opening as follows:
Row 1 Sl1 k-wise, rep from * to * on row 1 of cardigan twice,
then k1, p5, k4, turn and work on these sts for first side.
Row 2 and every alt row Sl1 k-wise, k1, p to last st, k1.
Row 3 Patt to last 10 sts, k1, p4, k2tog, k2, yf, k1.
Row 5 Patt to last 10 sts, k1, p3, k2tog, k2, yf, k2.
Row 7 Patt to last 10 sts, k1, p2, k2tog, k2, yf, k3.
Row 9 Patt to last 10 sts, k1, p1, k2tog, k2, yf, k4.
Row 10 As row 2.
Row 11 Sl1 k-wise, k to end.
Rep rows 10 and 11 until armholes are same depth as front
armholes, ending at neck edge.
Row 1 Cast off 9 [11, 13] sts, p to last st, k1.
Row 2 Cast off 8 [10, 12] sts, k to last 2 sts, k2tog.
Row 3 K2tog, p to last st, k1.
Rep rows 2 and 3 twice. Cast off the rem 8 [10, 12] sts.
Join yarn where sts were left and work second side as follows:
Row 1 Inc in first st, k2, p5, rep from * to * on row 1 of
patt of cardigan, to last 2 sts, k2.
Row 2 and every alt row Sl1 k-wise, p to last 2 sts, k2.

Row 3 Sl1 k-wise, yf, k2, ssk, p4, rep from * to * on row 3
of patt of cardigan, to last 2 sts, k2.
Row 5 Sl1 k-wise, k1, yf, k2, ssk, p3, patt to end.
Row 7 Sl1 k-wise, k2, yf, k2, ssk, p2, patt to end.
Row 9 Sl1 k-wise, k3, yf, k2, ssk, p1, patt to end.
Complete to match first side, reversing shapings.

SLEEVES

Using 2.75mm needles and yarn double, cast on
80 [90, 100] sts. Change to single yarn.
Work 4 rows in g st.
Change to 3.25mm needles and st st, inc 1 st at both ends of
next and every foll 6th row until there are 96 [106, 116] sts.
Cont if necessary until work measures 19cm/7½in from beg.

SHAPE TOP OF SLEEVE

Cast off 6 sts at beg of each of next 2 rows then k2tog at both
ends of every alt row until 46 [54, 62] sts rem. Cast off.
Work a second sleeve in the same way.

NECKBAND

Join shoulder seams. With RS facing, using 2.75mm needles,
pick up and k 17 [21, 25] sts along neck edge of left side of
back, 22 [26, 30] sts along shaped edge of front, the 15 sts
at centre, 22 [26, 30] sts along other side and 17 [21, 25] sts
along right back (*93 [109, 125] sts.*) Knit 2 rows. Cast off.

FINISHING

Block or press carefully, as given on page 137.
Join the side and sleeve seams. Sew in sleeves, placing seam
to seam. Using crochet hook, work a row of dc around the
back opening, making 3 buttonhole loops on the RH side
at equal distances (see page 139). Sew on buttons to match
buttonholes. Press seams.

Here is a really glamorous two-piece from the 1930s, knitted in cotton 4ply. The large leaf pattern is quick to knit and economical with yarn, which were both concerns for home knitters when the pattern was originally published. The skirt is knitted from the hem up and finished with elastic for a snug fit at the waist (see photograph on page 112); the hem is worked with a row of double crochet for a final touch. The softly draped unstructured blouse is typical of the period before the more tailored shapes of the 1940s.

Veronica Lacy Cotton Skirt & Top

Materials

YARN
5 x 100g balls Patons 100% cotton 4ply (100% mercerized cotton, approximately 330m/361 yards), shade 1729 Delta

NEEDLES
1 pair needles size 2.5mm
1 pair needles size 4.5mm
1 pair needles size 5mm
1 crochet hook size 3mm
1 crochet hook size 4mm

NOTIONS
Elastic for waistband

MEASUREMENTS
To fit Small [Medium, Large]
Top
Actual chest size 84 [94, 104]cm
33 [37, 41]in
Length to back neck 55 [58, 61]cm
21½ [22¾, 24]in
Skirt
Actual hip size 100 [110, 120]cm
39 [43, 47]in
Length 66cm/26in, adjustable

TENSION
26 stitches and 30 rows measure 10cm/4in over pattern on 4.5mm needles (or size needed to obtain given tension)

Top

BACK

Using 2.5mm needles, cast on 104 [116, 126] sts and work k2, p2 rib for 8cm/3in.

Work 1 row k, dec as follows:

Small Dec 1 st in every 5th st. *(92 sts.)*

Medium K9, k2tog, (k6, k2tog) 12 times, k to end. *(103 sts.)*

Large K7, k2tog, (k8, k2tog) 11 times, k to end. *(114 sts.)*

Work 1 row p.

Change to 5mm needles and work in patt as follows:

Row 1 K2, *k2tog, k3, yon, k1, yon, k3, skpo. Rep from * ending with k2.

Row 2 and all even rows Purl.

Row 3 K2, *k2tog, k2, yon, k3, yon, k2, skpo. Rep from * ending with k2.

Row 5 K2, *k2tog, k1, yon, k5, yon, k1, skpo. Rep from * ending with k2.

Row 7 K2, *k2tog, yon, k7, yon, skpo. Rep from * ending with k2.

Row 9 K1, k2tog, *yon, k4, k2tog, k3, yon, skpo. Rep from * ending with k1.

(**Note:** 91 [102, 113] sts on needle, rows 9–20 have 1 st less across row, which is regained on row 21.)

Row 11 K2, *yon, k3, skpo, k2tog, k3, yon, k1. Rep from * ending with yon, k2.

Row 13 K2, *yon, k3, skpo, k2tog, k3, yon, k1. Rep from * ending with yon, k2.

Row 15 K3, *yon, k2, skpo, k2tog, k2, yon, k3. Rep from * across row.

Row 17 K4, *yon, k1, skpo, k2tog, k1, yon, k5. Rep from * ending with yon, k4.

Row 19 K5, *yon, skpo, k2tog, yon, k7. Rep from * ending with yon, k5.

Row 21 K6, *yon, skpo, yon, k4, k2tog, k3. Rep from * ending with yon, k6. *(82 [103, 114] sts.)*

Row 22 Purl.

These 22 rows form the pattern.

Work in patt to 36 [38, 40]cm/14 [15, 15¾]in, ending after a RS row.

Cast on 22 sts (2 patts for sleeve), p across row, cast on 22 sts for other sleeve. *(125 [147, 158] sts.)*

Cont in patt until armhole measures 18 [19, 20]cm/ 7 [7½, 8]in; cast off loosely.

FRONT
Same as back.

JOIN UNDERARM SEAMS
Sew across 4 patts for each shoulder, leaving 4 patts for neck.
Using 4mm crochet hook, work 1 row dc around neck and sleeves (see page 139).

Skirt

Using 5mm needles, cast on 246 [268, 290] sts. (This is the bottom of the skirt.)

Work in lace patt as for top for 20cm/8in, change to 4.5mm needles and work to 61cm/24in or 5cm/2in less than desired length.

On last p row, p2tog (about every 5th and 6th st) until 208 sts rem.
Change to 2.5mm needles, work k2, p2 rib for 5cm/2in and cast off but do not break yarn.

Using 3mm crochet hook, work casing for elastic inside ribbing as follows: *ch5, miss 2 ribs, 1 slip st in next st at base of ribbing, ch5, miss 2 ribs, 1 slip st in next st at top of ribbing, rep from * around skirt.
Using 4mm crochet hook, work 1 row dc around hem of skirt. Fasten off.

FINISHING
Turn WS out, block carefully, as given on page 137; if damp, lay it on a flat surface until thoroughly dry.
Sew seams, matching patts. Insert elastic into casing at waist and sew ends together to suit.

Finishing Touches

Knitted accessories were extremely popular from the 1930s onwards, and knitted lace stockings (see page 126) were the height of fashion when silk stockings were virtually unobtainable. A Fair Isle beret (see page 122) would have been one item that every girl and young woman had in her possession; being highly fashionable and quick to knit from odd colours of yarn, it was appealing as well as practical. Wives and girlfriends of servicemen stationed in the Shetland Islands during the war might have received them as gifts, which only added to their popularity. Scarves and gloves of all styles were also knitted for all members of the family. We chose to include a design for a stole or large scarf that is inspired by a 1950s pattern (see page 118). Knitted in an openwork stitch and finished with a crochet trim, it is suitable for either day or evening. We also included some lacy wristwarmers (see page 130) that are quick to knit, as well as being pretty and warm – perfect for adding a finishing touch to any outfit.

The 1950s were the years when the stole was most fashionable — think Grace Kelly and Audrey Hepburn — and here we revive the style to be worn as a scarf or wrap. Instead of fringes, we have finished the ends with a pretty picot crochet edge in a contrast colour. The big needles used create a soft, airy fabric that will drape beautifully and work up quickly. A wool-cashmere blend makes it cosy to wear, and the yarn comes in a fabulous range of colours, so why not make several for different jackets?

Loretta Warm Lacy Stole

Materials

YARN

Rowan Cashsoft 4ply (57% extra fine merino, 33% acrylic microfibre, 10% cashmere, approximately 180m/197 yards):
7 x 50g balls, shade 430 Loganberry (A)
1 x 50g ball, shade 461 Jewel (B)

NEEDLES

1 pair needles size 5mm
1 crochet hook size 4mm

SPECIAL ABBREVIATION

ssk slip 1, slip 1, as if to knit, insert LH needle into front of these 2 sts from L to R, then knit together

MEASUREMENTS

Length 168cm/66in or desired length
Width approximately 40cm/16in when blocked

TENSION

Tension is not important for this item

Using 5mm needles and yarn B, cast on 67 sts.
Work 4 rows in g st.
Change to yarn A.
Row 1 Sl1, k2, (yf, ssk, k1, k2tog, yrn, p3) 7 times, yf, ssk, k1, k2tog, yf, k3.
Row 2 Sl1, k2, (p5, k3) 8 times.
Row 3 Sl1, k2, (k1, yf, k3tog, yf, k1, p3) 7 times, k1, yf, k3tog, yf, k4.
Row 4 As row 2.
These 4 rows form the pattern.
Rep these 4 rows until yarn A is used, or desired length is worked.
Using yarn B, work 4 rows in g st.
Cast off loosely, but do not break off yarn.

CROCHET EDGING

Using 4mm crochet hook, work crochet edge as follows (see page 139):
Row 1 (5ch, miss 2 sts, 1dc in next st) to end, work 3ch, 1tr in edge stitch, turn.
Row 2 (5ch, 1dc in loop) to end, turn.
Row 3 3ch, (2tr, 1ch, 3tr) in first loop, 1dc, *(3tr, 1ch, 3tr) in next loop, 1dc in next loop, rep from * to end.
Fasten off.
Rejoin yarn B to other end of stole and work crochet edging to match.

FINISHING

Block or press carefully, as given on page 137.

This retro Fair Isle beret is knitted in the real Shetland yarn that was used in the 1940s; the style would have been part of every girl's and woman's wardrobe during that era and could have been made in myriad different colour combinations. Knitted in the round, and using a chart, it is cleverly fastened off at the centre of the star. When you have finished it, block it on a plate of the correct size to get a beautifully shaped beret that will keep out the winter chill.

Kim Fair Isle Beret

Materials

YARN
Jamieson & Smith 2ply Jumper Weight (100%
Shetland wool, approximately 115m/125 yards):
2 x 25g balls, shade 043 Raspberry (A)
1 x 25g ball, shade 101 Pale Pink (B)
1 x 25g ball, shade 01A Off White (C)
1 x 25g ball shade 014 Pale Blue (D)

NEEDLES
Set of four double-pointed needles size 3mm

SPECIAL ABBREVIATION
sk2p slip 1, knit 2 together, pass slipped stitch over

MEASUREMENTS
One size

TENSION
30 stitches and 40 rows measure 10cm/4in over
pattern on 3mm needles (or size needed
to obtain given tension)

Note: Read every chart row from right to left.

Using yarn A and a set of 4 double-pointed needles size 3mm, cast on 160 sts (50, 60, 50) and with the 4th needle work in rounds of k1, p1 rib for 2.5cm/1in.

Next round (K3, inc in next st) to end. *(200 sts.)*

Rounds 1–3 Work chart 1.

Round 4 Using yarn A, (k9, inc in next st) to end.
Then work chart 2 (9 rounds).

Round 14 Using yarn A, (k10, inc in next st) to end. *(240 sts.)*
Work chart 2 (13 rounds).

Round 28 Using yarn A, (k4, k2tog) to end.
Repeat chart 2 (9 rounds).

Round 38 Using yarn A, (k3, k2tog) to end.
Work chart 4 (4 rounds).

Round 43 Using yarn A, (k2, k2tog) to end.
Work chart 5 (3 rounds).

Round 47 Using yarn A, (k4, k2tog) to end. *(100 sts.)*
Work chart 6, noting that the sts marked XXX are worked as follows: sk2p.
Work all rem charts, 7–12, working the sts marked XXX as on chart 6.

FINISHING
Run the end through rem sts, draw up and fasten off securely inside the beret.
Block or press carefully, as given on page 137.

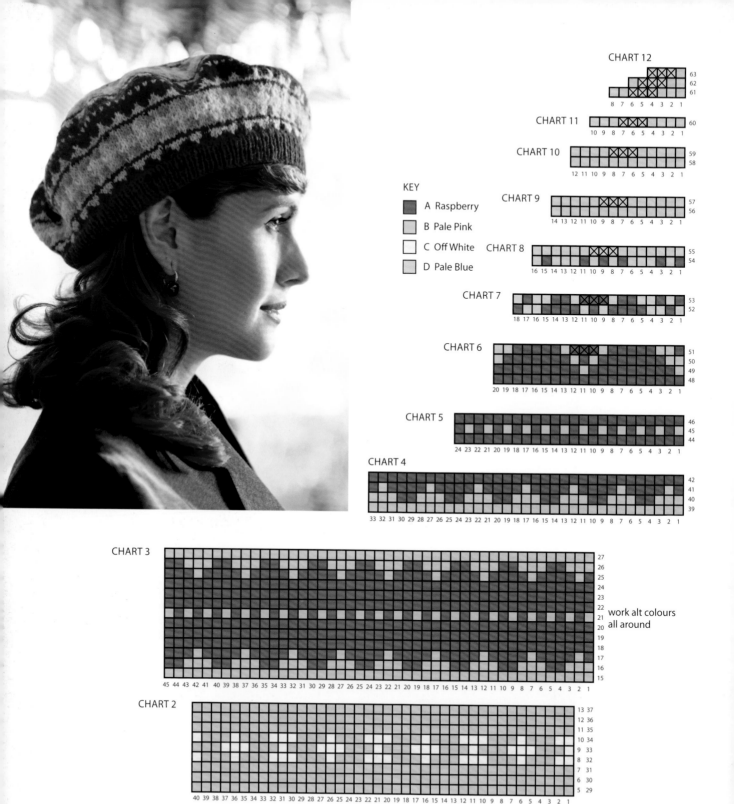

KEY

- ■ A Raspberry
- ■ B Pale Pink
- □ C Off White
- ■ D Pale Blue

work alt colours all around

Read all rows from right to left.

This is a pattern from the war years, which was sold advising the knitter to 'spin out the coupons' and knit her own stockings. We have chosen a yarn with a touch of mohair that will keep you warm and add glamour. These stockings are knitted on two needles, for those who find knitting in the round tricky. This also enhances the vintage look by creating a seam at the back.

Betty Lace Stockings

Materials

YARN
2 x 25g balls Bergere de France Angel
(44% polyamide, 32% acrylic, 24% mohair,
approximately 275m/300 yards),
shade 212.231 Pave

NEEDLES
I pair needles size 2.75mm
I pair needles size 3.75mm
Safety pins

MEASUREMENTS
To fit 23cm/9in foot
Length of leg from bottom of heel 59cm/27in

TENSION
26 stitches and 32 rows measure 10cm/4in over
pattern on 3.75mm needles (or size needed to
obtain given tension)

Note: If you don't want to wear the suspender belt
these stockings were designed for, you will have to
thread a little elastic around the ribbing at the top.

TOP OF STOCKING
Using 3.75mm needles and yarn double, cast on 96 sts.
Break off one thread of yarn and cont in single yarn.
Row I *K2, p2, rep from * to end.
Cont in rib until 10cm/4in of rib have been worked.
Next row Rib 2, *work 2tog, rib 4, rep from * to last
4 sts, work 2tog, rib 2. *(80 sts.)*
Commence patt as follows:
Row I KI, *yf, k2tog, rep from * to last st, kI.
Row 2 KI, purl to last st, kI.
Row 3 KI, *k2tog, yf, rep from * to last st, kI.
Row 4 KI, purl to last st, kI.
These 4 rows form the pattern.
Rep rows I–4 until work measures 20cm/8in.
Change to 2.75mm needles and cont until work measures
25cm/10in from beg, finishing at end of a 4th row.
If a longer or shorter stocking is required, adjust
measurement at this point, still finishing at end of a 4th row.

SHAPE LEG
Row I KI, *yf, k2tog, rep from * to last st, kI.
Row 2 KI, p2tog twice, purl to last 5 sts, p2tog twice, kI.
Row 3 KI, *k2tog, yf, rep from * to last st, kI.
Row 4 KI, purl to last st, kI.
Rep rows I–4 once.
Row 9 As row I.
Row 10 As row 4.
Rows 11 and 12 As rows 3 and 4.
Rows 13 and 14 As rows I and 4.
Rows 15 and 16 As rows 3 and 8.
Cont shaping on every 8th row to 52 sts.
Rep rows I–4 of original patt rows until work measures
52cm/20½in from the beg, finishing at end of a row 4.

If a narrower leg is required, change to a size smaller needles. If any change to length measurement was made previously, adjust this measurement to correspond.

Now work as follows:

Row 1 K3, *yf, k2tog, rep from * to last 3 sts, k3.

Row 2 and every alt row K1, p to last st, k1.

Row 3 K3, *k2tog, yf, rep from * to last 3 sts, k3.

Row 5 K5, *yf, k2tog, rep from * to last 5 sts, k5.

Row 7 K5, *k2tog, yf, rep from * to last 5 sts, k5.

Row 9 K7, *yf, k2tog, rep from * to last 7 sts, k7.

Row 11 K7, *k2tog, yf, rep from * to last 7 sts, k7.

Row 13 K9, *yf, k2tog, rep from * to last 9 sts, k9.

Row 15 K9, *k2tog, yf, rep from * to last 9 sts, k9.

Row 17 K11, *yf, k2tog, rep from * to last 11 sts, k11.

Row 19 K11, *k2tog, yf, rep from * to last 11 sts, k11.

Row 21 K13, *yf, k2tog, rep from * to last 13 sts, k13.

Row 23 K13, *k2tog, yf, rep from * to last 13 sts, k13.

Row 24 K1, p to last st, k1.

Divide for heel as follows:

Next row K15, *yf, k2tog, rep from * to last 15 sts, k1. Slip rem 14 sts onto first safety pin, turn.

Next row K1, p to last 15 sts, k1. Slip rem 14 sts onto second safety pin, turn.

Proceed on former set of 24 sts for instep as follows: Commencing with a 3rd row of patt, rep original patt rows for 14cm/5½in or length required, ending with WS facing for next row.

Next row K1, inc in next st, *p2, inc in next st, rep from * to last st, k1. *(32 sts.)*

SHAPE TOE

Row 1 K1, skpo, k to last 3 sts, k2tog, k1.

Row 2 K1, p to last st, k1.

Rep rows 1 and 2 ten times more. *(10 sts.)*

Break off yarn. Slip sts onto third safety pin.

With RS facing, slip sts from first safety pin onto an empty needle, then slip them onto second empty needle, thus the point will be to the outside.

Now slip sts from second safety pin onto needle containing the 14 sts, thus RS will be facing when working next row.

Join yarn and proceed as follows:

Row 1 Knit.

Row 2 K1, p to last st, k1.

Rep rows 1 and 2 fifteen times more.

SHAPE HEEL

Row 1 K15, k2tog, k1, turn.

Row 2 P4, p2tog, p1, turn.

Row 3 K5, k2tog, k1, turn.

Row 4 P6, p2tog, p1, turn.

Cont in this manner, working 1 st more on every row until the row 'p14, p2tog, p1' has been worked. Break off yarn.

With RS facing and commencing at point where instep and heel divide, join yarn and, using empty needle, k up 18 sts along one side of heel, k across 16 sts on second needle, then k up 18 sts along second side of heel. *(52 sts.)*

Dec as follows:

Row 1 K1, p to last st, k1.

Row 2 K1, skpo, k to last 3 sts, k2tog, k1.

Rows 3–20 Rep rows 1 and 2 nine times. *(32 sts.)*

Cont in st st without further shaping until work measures 14cm/5½in from point where sts were knitted up at heel, finishing at end of a p row.

SHAPE TOE

Work as instructions for piece first worked, slipping toe sts from safety pin onto full needle. Graft or cast off together the two sets of sts (see page 138).

Make another stocking to match.

FINISHING

Block or press carefully, as given on page 137. Neatly stitch the foot and leg seams, taking care to make a flat seam.

What could be more useful than these pretty wristwarmers knitted in a lacy stitch in cosy double-knitting wool? They are so quick to knit, using only one ball of yarn, that you are bound to wonder if one pair will be enough. When were wristwarmers invented? No one seems to know, but fingerless gloves have been worn since Victorian days up to the present time, and wristwarmers are their natural cousins: practical and warm and — in the case of our pattern — rather cheeky.

Greta Lacy Wristwarmers

Materials

YARN
1 x 50g ball Artesano Soft Merino Superwash DK (100% merino wool, approximately 112m/120 yards), shade 5167 Teal

NEEDLES
1 pair needles size 3.25mm
1 pair needles size 4mm

MEASUREMENTS
One size
Length 20cm/8in
Around hand 20cm/8in

TENSION
22 stitches and 28 rows measure 10cm/4in over stocking stitch on 4mm needles (or size needed to obtain given tension)

Using 3.25mm needles, cast on 40 sts and work cuff
as follows:
Row 1 P1, (k2, p2) 9 times, k2, p1.
Row 2 K1, (p2, k2) 9 times, p2, k1.
Rep these 2 rows to 5cm/2in.
Change to 4mm needles and work as follows:
Row 1 K19, *yf, k2tog, rep from * to last st, k1.
Row 2 K1, p to last st, k1.
Row 3 K19, *k2tog, yf, rep from * to last st, k1.
Row 4 K1, p to last st, k1.
These 4 rows form the pattern.
Rep these 4 rows for 12cm/5in.
Change to 3.25mm needles and work in rib, as for cuff,
for 2.5cm/1in. Cast off.

Make another wristwarmer to match but working 2.5cm/
1in rib at the beginning and 5cm/2in at the end.
(**Note:** the second wristwarmer is worked upside down,
then there is no need to work out how many stitches to
do in pattern before the st st.)

FINISHING
Block or press carefully, as given on page 137.
Sew side seam, leaving 5cm/2in open for thumb 8cm/3in
from the start of the cuff.

Techniques

TENSION

A tension guide is given at the beginning of a pattern – for example, 22 stitches and 30 rows measure 10cm/4in over stocking stitch on 4mm needles. This tells you how large the stitches are on the garment, so that, by matching this tension, you can produce a garment the correct size. Four factors affect tension: needle size, stitch pattern, yarn and the knitter.

NEEDLE SIZE

Generally speaking, larger needles produce larger stitches and smaller needles produce smaller stitches. Needle brand and what the needle is made of can also affect tension; in addition, some have sharper points than others.

STITCH PATTERN

Different stitch patterns produce different tensions, therefore you must check your tension using the stitch pattern specified each time you embark on a new pattern.

YARN

Patterns worked in finer yarns have more stitches and rows over 10cm/4in than those worked in thicker yarns. It is very important to check your tension if you use a different yarn from that specified in the pattern, as even a standard weight of yarn can vary from one manufacturer to another.

THE KNITTER

Even when using the same yarn, needle size and stitch pattern, two knitters may not produce knitting at the same tension. If your tension does not match that given in the pattern, you should change to a larger or smaller needle size.

ABBREVIATIONS

( )	repeat all the instructions between brackets as many times as indicated	k2togtbl	knit 2 stitches together through back loops	RH	right hand
		k-wise	knitwise	RS	right side
[ ]	figures in square brackets refer to larger sizes	L	left	skpo	slip 1, k1, pass slipped stitch over
		LH	left hand		
0	no stitches, rows or times	m1	make 1 st as follows: pick up loop lying between needles and k tbl	sl	slip
(00 sts.)	number of stitches, denotes the number of stitches you should have on your needle(s) at this point			slip st	crochet, insert hook in next st, yarn over and draw through both loops on hook
		mm	millimetre(s)		
		moss st	k1, p1 on an odd number of stitches	ssk	slip 1, slip 1, as if to knit, insert LH needle into front of these 2 sts from L to R, then knit together
alt	alternate(ly)				
beg	begin(ning)	p	purl		
ch	crochet chain st	p2tog	purl 2 stitches together		
cm	centimetre(s)	p2togtbl	purl 2 stitches together through back loops	st(s)	stitch(es)
cont	continu(e)(ing)(ity)			st st	stocking stitch
dc	double crochet	patt	pattern	tbl	through back loop(s)
dec	decreas(e)(ing)	psso	pass slipped stitch over	tog	together
foll	following	p-wise	purlwise	WS	wrong side
g	gram(s)	R	right	wyif	with yarn in/at front
g st	garter stitch	rem	remain(ing)	ybk	yarn back
in	inch(es)	rep	repeat	yf	yarn forward
inc	increas(e)(ing)	rep from *	repeat all the instructions that follow the asterisk as many times as indicated	yon	yarn over needle
k	knit			yrn	yarn round needle
k2tog	knit 2 stitches together				

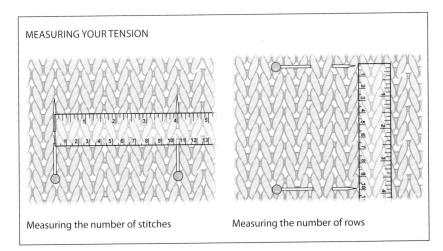

MEASURING YOUR TENSION

Measuring the number of stitches

Measuring the number of rows

MAKING A TENSION SAMPLE

Using the yarn, needles and stitch pattern called for, knit a sample slightly larger than 10cm/4in square. Block the sample as the finished garment would be blocked (see instructions on page 137).

Being careful not to stretch it, place the sample right side up on a flat surface and place a rigid ruler along one row. Use pins to mark the beginning and end of a 10cm/4in measurement. Count the number of stitches between the pins.

Then place the ruler vertically along one side of a column of stitches, and mark your 10cm/4in measurement as before. Count the number of rows between the pins.

If you have fewer stitches and rows than given in the pattern, you should use a smaller needle; if there are more stitches and rows, then you should try a larger needle. As a rough guide, changing the needle one size makes a difference of about one stitch in every 5cm/2in.

If you cannot match both the stitch and row tension, work to the correct stitch tension, as the length can be adjusted by working more or fewer rows. Or, if you are not getting enough rows, use a size smaller needle only on the purl side.

SPECIAL TECHNIQUES

Some of the patterns in this book require you to follow colour charts, and knit with two colours of yarn in a row. Here is some helpful information on these techniques.

KNITTING IN THE ROUND

In this book, the *Kim* Fair Isle Beret (see page 122) is knitted in the round. This has the advantage that the front of the work always faces you, so it is easier to follow colour-pattern charts.

Circular needles or a set of double-pointed needles are used; if you are using circular needles, you cast on in the usual way, do not turn the work but knit

into the first stitch to make a continuous round. You must make certain that your cast-on row is not twisted when commencing your first round. To knit stocking stitch, simply knit every row.

If you are using a set of four double-pointed needles, the stitches are divided among three of the needles, and the fourth is used to knit. To close the circle, knit into the first cast-on stitch, marking this stitch with contrasting-colour thread, and making sure no gap forms in the knitting. If you find it difficult to avoid gaps when changing from one needle to another, you can rotate these points around the work by moving two or three stitches each time you change from one needle to another.

COLOUR-PATTERN CHARTS

Colour patterns are often given in the form of a chart, where each square represents one stitch and each line of the chart represents one row.

The chart is worked from bottom to top, and the rows are usually numbered with odd numbers on the right-hand side of the chart and even numbers on the left. The same chart is used for circular or flat knitting, although it must be read differently.

In circular knitting, every row on the chart represents a round of knitting; since you have the right side

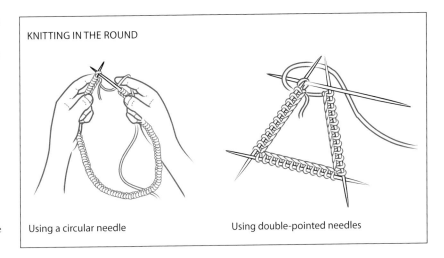

KNITTING IN THE ROUND

Using a circular needle

Using double-pointed needles

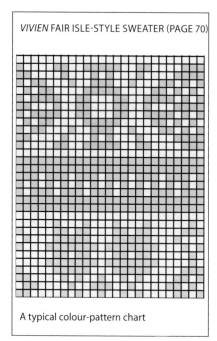

VIVIEN FAIR ISLE-STYLE SWEATER (PAGE 70)

A typical colour-pattern chart

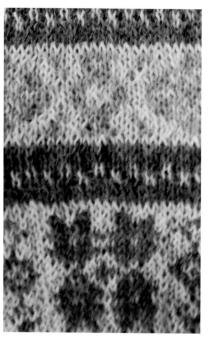

of the work facing you, every stitch will be a knit stitch and you read every row from right to left.

For flat knitting, you will knit backwards and forwards in stocking stitch, so the first row (and odd-numbered rows) will be knit and the chart read from right to left; these are right-side rows. The second row (and every even-numbered row) is worked in purl and the chart read from left to right; these are wrong-side rows.

USING TWO COLOURS OF YARN IN A ROW
When knitting with two colours of yarn in a row, the yarn that is not being used has to be carried across the back of the knitting. This is normally done by stranding (see right). The advantage of stranding is that the finished fabric is softer than that achieved with weaving in; when using this method it is very important that the strands at the back of the work are not pulled too tightly, both to achieve the correct tension and to retain the natural give in the finished fabric. To ensure this, every time you change colour, gently but firmly pull

back the last ten or so stitches on the right-hand needle, so that your knitting is very slightly stretched.

WEAVING IN
If there are more than five stitches between colour changes, you should use the weaving-in method so that there are not long loops at the back of the work. Knit two stitches as normal, then lift the non-working colour onto the tip of the right-hand

needle before knitting the strand as though it were part of the stitch, but letting the strand fall back behind the working colour, and continue with the main colour only for another one or two stitches. Repeat this, keeping the floats loose, but not slack, until you are ready to take up the next colour.

If you need to weave in your main colour, insert the right needle into the stitch, wind the non-working yarn around the needle as if to knit it, then wind the working yarn around the needle in the usual way. Take the non-working yarn back behind the working yarn, and complete the knitted stitch.

Stranding and weaving can also be done on purl rows where necessary.

INTARSIA KNITTING
The *Hedy* Tyrolean-Pattern Cardigan (see page 46) requires a method of knitting called intarsia, which is used for working a block pattern on a plain background. In this pattern, three colours are used in a row, the background colour and two contrast colours. Where the colours change over at the edge of the pattern, the yarns are twisted around one another to prevent holes from forming. Only the background colour is carried across the row. In the block pattern, the contrast colours are woven in (see above).

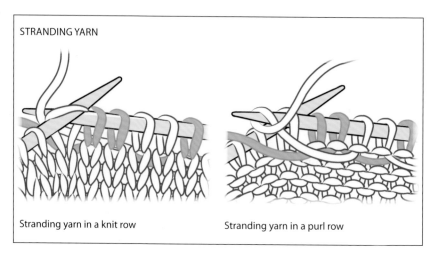

STRANDING YARN

Stranding yarn in a knit row

Stranding yarn in a purl row

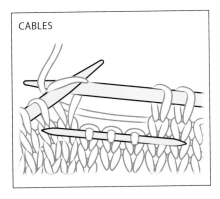

CABLES

CABLES

These are created when stitches are moved out of position, so that plaited, rope-like twists are formed. This is achieved by using a special, double-pointed cable needle.

A given number of stitches are slipped onto the cable needle and held at either the front or back of the work. A number of stitches are then worked from the main needle, followed by the stitches on the cable needle.

Stitches held at the front twist a cable to the left when knitted off; stitches held at the back twist the cable to the right when knitted off.

JOINING IN NEW YARN

Try to avoid joining a new ball of yarn in the middle of a row or round. To judge whether the remaining length of yarn is long enough to complete the row or round, use this rough guideline: in stocking stitch, each row or round takes about three times the width of the knitting. In cable or texture knitting the yarn needed is about five times the width of the knitting.

To join at the beginning of a row, break off the old yarn leaving a few centimetres of spare yarn; join the new colour and the finished colour with a single knot, making sure the knot is close to the last stitch on your right-hand needle. Begin the next row and weave the spare yarn into the first ten stitches of the round, before

carefully trimming away the excess. Alternatively, this can be done at the finishing stage, using a darning needle.

BUTTONHOLES

A basic horizontal buttonhole is made by casting off the required number of stitches on the right-side row, and casting them on again on the return row. It is slightly neater if the first cast-on stitch is worked as an increase in the last stitch before casting on the others, plus one, which is knitted together with the next stitch.

BEADS

Before you start knitting the sleeves or the band of the *Ava* Angora Bolero (see page 52 and detail below), the beads need to be threaded onto the yarn. Thread a needle that will easily pass through the bead with doubled sewing cotton, so that there are cut ends on one side and a loop at the other. Pass the yarn through the loop (double yarn in the case of the bolero in this book), and thread the required number of beads down the needle and onto the yarn.

To place the bead in the work so that it appears on the right side, knit to the position of the bead, bring the yarn forward, position the bead, slip the stitch purlwise, take the yarn back and knit the next stitch.

FINISHING

When you have finished knitting, the garment pieces have to be blocked and sewn together.

BLOCKING

Pin each garment piece out on a flat surface to the correct measurements. The blocking surface can be a firm base, such as the floor or a table, covered with a blanket or towel, with a cotton sheet or a piece of checked cloth, which you can use as a guide to keep the edges straight, placed on top. Spray the knitting with cold, clean water, using a plant spray, until it is damp, but not soaked, and leave it to dry naturally.

For cotton garments, pin out each piece to size and then lightly press them using a steam iron or a damp cloth and a regular iron. Do not move the iron across the fabric, as this will stretch it, but press it gently with up-and-down movements.

Lace knitting is very delicate, but it does need careful blocking in order to obtain the openwork effect. In this case, lay the lace knitting on your blocking surface and dampen it lightly. Then very gently ease it to the correct size, so that it is slightly stretched, and leave it to dry naturally.

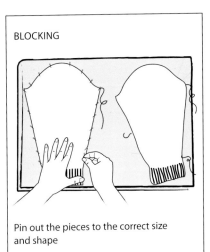

BLOCKING

Pin out the pieces to the correct size and shape

SEWING TOGETHER

The most versatile stitch for sewing up the pieces of your garment is mattress stitch, which provides a strong, invisible seam.

Start by placing the two seam edges side by side, with right sides facing you. Using a tapestry needle and the same yarn as you used to knit the garment, stitch through two horizontal threads, one stitch in from the edge on one side. Pick up the two corresponding threads one stitch in on the other side. Without pulling the stitches taut, pick up the next two threads on the first side. Then go back to the other side and pick up the next two threads, and so on.

When the thread is looped from one edge to the other about five times, pull it taut and the seam will be pulled together. Continue until the seam is complete.

GRAFTING OR KITCHENER STITCH

With the stitches on the needles and both points facing to the right, place the two sets of stitches together with the wrong sides of the work facing and a length of yarn at the right-hand end.

Thread the yarn through a yarn needle, *insert the yarn needle through the first stitch as if to knit, draw the yarn through and slip the stitch off, insert the yarn needle in the next stitch as if to purl, draw the yarn through and leave the stitch on the needle, take the yarn under the front needle and insert the yarn needle as if to purl into the first stitch on the back needle, draw the yarn through and slip the stitch off the needle, insert the yarn needle as if to knit into the next stitch, draw the yarn through leaving the stitch on the needle, bring to the front needle again, and rep from * until all the stitches are worked off.

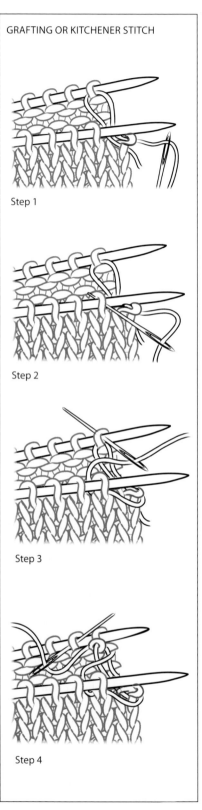

GRAFTING OR KITCHENER STITCH

Step 1

Step 2

Step 3

Step 4

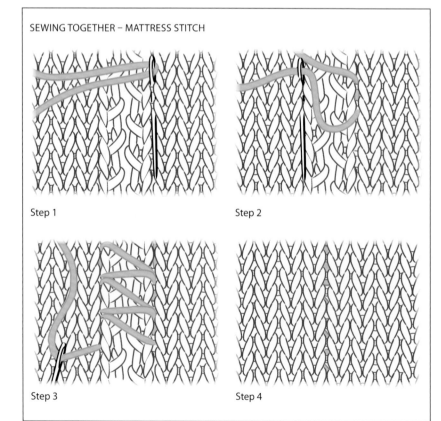

SEWING TOGETHER – MATTRESS STITCH

Step 1

Step 2

Step 3

Step 4

CROCHET EDGES

Some patterns require you to work a row or two of crochet along an edge. Unless specified in the pattern, use a size hook equal to the needle size used for the ribbing, or one or two sizes smaller than for the main section. Work one double crochet into three out of every four row ends, then, if required, work one more row of one double crochet in each double crochet to the end.

WASHING

After spending a lot of time and trouble hand-knitting a sweater, it pays to wash it with care. A lot of yarns now may be safely machine-washed, but always check the ball band of the yarn for washing instructions in case hand-washing is specified, and keep one band for reference.

For those items that must be hand-washed, use a wool detergent and hand-warm water. Gently immerse the garment and squeeze it in the suds for a few minutes. Do not rub or soak the garment. Rinse in the same temperature of water several times to remove all the detergent and until the rinse water is absolutely clear. Place the garment on a thick towel and roll both up. Press the roll with your hands to remove as much water as possible.

Alternatively, put the garment in a tied pillowcase and give it a very short, fast spin in a washing machine. (This avoids it being stretched around the drum of the machine.) Then spread the damp garment on a clean towel on a rack over the bath, easing it to the correct size and shape, and allow it to dry naturally. Do not spin delicate yarns such as those that include cashmere.

Never store knitted garments on a hanger. Always keep them folded flat in a drawer or on a shelf.

Beware of moths – make sure your knitted garments are clean before storing them for long periods, and use a moth repellent.

Directory of Garments

Below is a directory of all the garments featured in this book, from pretty short-sleeved summer tops that look great with skirts and jeans, cosy cover-ups for cooler days and glamorous sweaters that evoke the elegance of a bygone age, to cute accessories that make perfect finishing touches to any outfit.

Jayne Button-Front Top 16

Bette Top with Keyhole Neckline 20

Doris Shell Top 24

Shirley Lace Top 28

Louise Latticework Jersey 32

Marilyn Magyar Top 36

Kate Lace-Panel Blouse 40

Hedy Tyrolean-Pattern Cardigan 46

Ava Angora Bolero 52

Lauren Lace-Stitch Cardigan 56

Wallis Pleated Cardigan 60

Clara Bow-Panel Sweater 66

Vivien Fair Isle-Style Sweater 70

Grace Lacy Puff-Sleeve Sweater 76

Marlene Lacy Sweater with Collar 80

Audrey Leaf-Pattern Sweater 84

Natalie Feather-Stitch Sweater 88

Barbara Fine Cable Twinset 96

Celia Lacy Fine-Knit Twinset 102

Veronica Lacy Cotton Skirt & Top 108

Loretta Warm Lacy Stole 118

Kim Fair Isle Beret 122

Betty Lace Stockings 126

Greta Lacy Wristwarmers 130

Resources

BUTTON SUPPLIERS

Duttons for Buttons
Oxford Street
Harrogate
North Yorkshire
HG1 1QE
+44 (0)1423 502092
michelle@duttonsforbuttons.co.uk
www.duttonsforbuttons.co.uk

BEADS

Debbie Abrahams Beads
26 Church Drive
Nottingham
NG5 2BA
+44 (0)115 855179
beads@debbieabrahams.com
www.debbieabrahamsbeads.co.uk

YARNS

Adriafil of Italy
contact@adriafil.com
www.adriafil.com/uk
to find your nearest stockist

Artesano Ltd
Unit G, Lamb's Farm Business Park
Basingstoke Road
Swallowfield
Reading
Berkshire
RG7 1PQ
+44 (0)118 9503350
www.artesanoyarns.co.uk
to find your nearest stockist

Cucumberpatch Ltd
63 High Street
Wolstanton
Newcastle-under-Lyme
Staffs
ST5 8BB
+44 (0)1782 862332
sales@cucumberpatch.co.uk
www.cucumberpatch.co.uk
for Artesano, Rowan, Wendy

Deramores Retail Ltd
Units 5–9 Tomas Seth Business Park
Argent Road
Queenborough
ME11 5TS
+44 (0)845 519 4573
www.deramores.com
for Patons, Sublime, Wendy

Designer Yarns Ltd
Unit 8–10 Newbridge Industrial Estate
Pitt Street
Keighley
West Yorkshire
BD21 4PQ
+44 (0)1535 664222
enquiries@designeryarns.uk.com
www.designeryarns.uk.com
for Louisa Harding

English Yarns Ltd
19 East Street
Shoreham-by-Sea
West Sussex
BN43 5ZE
+44 (0)1273 461029
sales@englishyarns.co.uk
www.englishyarns.co.uk
for Rowan, Sublime

Fyberspates Ltd
Unit 6 Oxleaze Farm Workshops
Broughton Poggs
Filkins
Lechlade
Glos
GL7 3RB
+44 (0)7540 656660
fyberspates@btinternet.com
www.fyberspates.co.uk

InToKnit.co.uk
28 Gapstile Close
Desbeau Park
Desborough
Northants
NN14 2TZ
+44 (0)845 8383 762
shop@intoknit.co.uk
www.bergere.co.uk
www.intoknit.co.uk
for Bergere de France

Jamieson & Smith (Shetland Wool Brokers) Ltd
90 North Road
Lerwick
Shetland Isles
ZE1 0PQ
+44 (0)1595 693579
sales@shetlandwoolbrokers.co.uk
www.shetlandwoolbrokers.co.uk

John Lewis
300 Oxford Street
London
W1A 1EX
+44 (0)20 7629 7711
www.johnlewis.com
for Artesano Superfine Alpaca, Fyberspates Scrumptious, Patons, Rowan

Laughing Hens
The Croft Stables
Station Lane
Great Barrow
Cheshire
CH3 7JN
+44 (0)1829 740903
sales@laughinghens.com
www.laughinghens.com
for Fyberspates Scrumptious, Louisa Harding, Patons, Rowan

Acknowledgements

Les Tricoteuses
12 Chapel Yard
Albert Street
Holt
Norfolk
NR25 6HG
info@lestricoteuses.co.uk
*for Bergere de France, Debbie Bliss, Louisa Harding,
Fyberspates, Artesano*

Orkney Angora
William & Elizabeth Sichel
Isle of Sanday
Orkney
Scotland
KW17 2AZ
+44 (0)1857 600421
info@orkneyangora.co.uk
www.orkneyangora.co.uk

Outback Yarns
130–132 King Street
Castle Douglas
Kirkcudbrightshire
DG7 1LU
+44 (0)1556 504900
OutbackYarns@btinternet.com
www.outbackyarns.co.uk
for Adriafil Avantgarde, Patons, Rowan, Wendy

Rowan Yarns
Green Lane Mill
Holmfirth
HD9 2DX
+44 (0)1484 681881
www.knitrowan.com
to find your nearest stockist

For all wallpapers featured in the book,
as seen at Mapesbury Road location
house, contact Marianne Cotterill at
www.mariannecotterill.com.

We have enjoyed working together as co-authors –
searching through vintage patterns, choosing yarns, and
generally talking about fashion history. We feel it has
been a very successful collaboration and we hope you will
enjoy knitting these patterns as much as we have enjoyed
preparing the book.

We thank everyone at Jacqui Small Publishing who nursed
this project through all its stages, especially Zia Mattocks
and Kerenza Swift. Thanks also to Barbara Zuñiga, Art
Director, Marianne Cotterill, Stylist, Victoria Barnes,
Make-up Artist, and Debi Treloar, Photographer, who have
produced beautiful shots that show off the knitwear so well.

With many thanks to all the knitters who worked to
complete garments in time for approaching deadlines:

Paulette Burgess
Joyce Coombs
Pat Cooper
Maria Courtenay-Luck
Hilary Grundy
Jackie Hall
Lindsey Kennedy Smith
Audrey Lincoln
Jean Molloy
Helen Scott
Mhairi Sinclair
Rita Taylor

Our thanks go to the following yarn companies who very
generously supplied complimentary yarn for the projects
in this book:

Artesano
Bergere de France
Orkney Angora
Sirdar/Sublime

Thanks also to Duttons for Buttons for supplying buttons.

To Les Tricoteuses for supplying yarns for sampling.

To *Knit Today* magazine for allowing us to use the pattern
for the *Doris* Shell Top on page 24.

To Naomi Leeds of *Knit* magazine for sending back copies.

*The publisher would like to thank Clements Ribeiro and Lyn Dennison
for the kind loan of clothes and shoes for photography.*